CALVIN AND HOBBES SUNDAY PAGES 1985-1995

An Exhibition Catalogue by

BILL WATTERSON

Andrews McMeel
Publishing

Kansas City

In cooperation with
The Ohio State University
Cartoon Research Library

For information, write Andrews McMeel Publishing, an Andrews McMeel Universal company, 4520 Main Street, Kansas City, Missouri 64111.

01 02 03 04 05 BAD 10 9 8 7 6 5 4 3 2 1

Library of Congress Cataloging-in-Publication Data
Watterson, Bill.
[Calvin and Hobbes. Selections]
Calvin and Hobbes : Sunday papers, 1985-1995 / Bill Watterson.
p. cm.
Catalog of an exhibition held Sept. 10, 2001 to Jan. 16, 2002 at the Ohio State University Cartoon Research Library.
Highlights 36 Sunday cartoons that the author has personally selected from his collection.
ISBN: 0-7407-2135-6
1. Watterson, Bill. Calvin and Hobbes–Exhibitions. 2. Watterson, Bill–Exhibitions. I. Title

PN6728.C34W385162001
741.5'973–dc21 2001046405

Design: Frank Pauer

This catalogue accompanies the exhibition *Calvin and Hobbes: Sunday Pages 1985-1995* at The Ohio State University Cartoon Research Library from September 10, 2001, to January 15, 2002.

The exhibition was mounted with the support of The Ohio State University Libraries. All works in the exhibition are from the personal collection of the cartoonist, and we are grateful to him for lending them for this purpose. We also appreciate the contributions of Frank Pauer, Marilyn Scott, Erin Shipley, Dennis Toth, Rick VanBrimmer, and Richard Samuel West to the exhibit and this publication. Special thanks to Andrews McMeel Publishing for producing and distributing this book.

Cover: [unpublished watercolor of Calvin and Hobbes] Private collection. Watercolor on paper. 12 x 12.4 cm.

PREFACE

Everyone misses *Calvin and Hobbes*.

It reinvented the newspaper comic strip at a time when many had all but buried the funnies as a vehicle for fresh, creative work. Then Bill Watterson came along and reminded a new generation of what older readers and comic strip afficionados knew: A well-written and beautifully drawn strip is an intricate, powerful form of communication. And with *Calvin and Hobbes*, we had fun—just like readers of *Krazy Kat* and *Pogo* did. Opening the newspaper each day was an adventure. The heights of Watterson's creative imagination took us places we had never been. We miss that.

This book is published in conjunction with the first exhibition of original *Calvin and Hobbes* Sunday pages at The Ohio State University Cartoon Research Library. Although the work was created for reproduction, not for gallery display, it is a pleasure to see the cartoonist's carefully placed lines and exquisite brush strokes. In an attempt to share this experience with those who are unable to visit the exhibition, all of the original Sunday pages displayed are reproduced in color in this book so that every detail, such as sketch lines, corrections, and registration marks, are visible. On the opposite page the same comic strip is printed in full color. Because Watterson was unusually intentional and creative in his use of color, this juxtaposition provides *Calvin and Hobbes* readers the opportunity to consider the impact of color on its narrative and content.

When I first contacted Bill Watterson about the possibility of exhibiting his original work, I used the term "retrospective." He replied that we might be able to do an exhibit, but that calling it a retrospective made him uncomfortable since it has been only a few years since he stopped drawing the comic strip. He felt that a longer time was needed to put *Calvin and Hobbes* in the historical perspective implied by that term. Nonetheless, this show is a "look back" at the comic strip as we revisit favorites that we remember. *Calvin and Hobbes: Sunday Pages 1985-1995* is particularly interesting because each work that is included was selected by Bill Watterson. His comments about the thirty-six Sunday pages he chose are part of this volume. In addition, he reflects on *Calvin and Hobbes* from the perspective of six years, and his essay provides insights into his life as a syndicated cartoonist.

Reprint books of *Calvin and Hobbes* are nice to have, but the opportunity to see the original work and read Bill Watterson's thoughts about it is a privilege. He generously shared not only the art, but also his time and his thoughts. When I first reviewed the works included in the exhibit, I knew that everyone who visited it would begin with laughter and end with tears.

On behalf of all who enjoyed *Calvin and Hobbes*, thank you, Bill Watterson.

Lucy Shelton Caswell
Professor and Curator
The Ohio State University Cartoon Research Library
June 2001

CALVIN AND HOBBES SUNDAY PAGES 1985-1995

It's been five years since the end of *Calvin and Hobbes*, the longest time I can remember in which I haven't drawn cartoons. *Calvin and Hobbes* was a wonderful experience, but it was an all-consuming career. When I quit the strip, I put my cartoons in boxes, and jumped into other interests. I haven't really considered the strip since, so at the invitation to do this show, I thought it might be time to look back at some of my work.

My first reaction in going through my old cartoons was some amazement at the size and weight of the pile. For most successful comic strips, ten years is just a drop in the bucket, but even that amount of time yields a huge amount of material. It's no wonder that decade seems like a blur.

Going through my old strips is sort of like looking at old photographs of myself: they're personal and familiar, yet somewhat bizarre at the same time. There are cartoons I've drawn that are the equivalent of pictures of my younger self wearing yellow pants: I know I'm responsible for that, but what on earth was I thinking? As my tastes have changed, and as I've learned more, I imagine that I would do many strips quite differently today. Not better necessarily, but certainly differently. I was twenty-eight when *Calvin and Hobbes* was first published, and, of course, I would make other choices now at age forty-three.

It's also sort of strange to see a record of my own learning curve. Pick up a given strip, and I see how I struggled with various writing and drawing problems, or how I finally surmounted one. I remember sometimes feeling that the strip was better written than I could actually write, and better drawn than I could actually draw. I learned a great deal over the years by trying to push the strip beyond my own abilities, and I'm very proud that *Calvin and Hobbes* explored and developed all the way to the end. By the final years, I see naturalness or a sense of inevitability to the drawing and writing that is very satisfying. I'm more appreciative of this kind of grace since returning to the awkward stages of new learning curves.

Of course, I'd also say the times have caught up with some of my strips. It's frankly a little discouraging to see how ordinary some of them look now. When *Calvin and Hobbes* first appeared, it was somewhat surprising to treat reality as subjective, and to draw a strip with multiple viewpoints, juxtaposing Calvin's vision with what others saw. I did this simply as a way to put the reader in Calvin's head and to reveal his imaginative personality. Now these juxtapositions are a visual game for many comic strips, and after all these years, I suspect readers know where this sort of joke is headed as soon as they see it. The novelty cannot be recaptured.

Novelty, however, is probably overrated anyway. The *Calvin and Hobbes* strips that hold up best, to my eye anyway, are the ones where the characters seem big, vivid, and full of life, and where the strip's world seems genuine and inviting. Punchlines come and go, but something in the friendship between Calvin and Hobbes seems to hold a small piece of truth. Expressing something real and honest is, for me, the joy and the importance of cartooning.

The Sunday strips were usually the cartoons I had the most fun with, and for this show I've chosen a few Sunday strips from each year that I think show off the strip's strengths.

I have fond memories of reading the Sunday comics when I was a kid. As far as I was concerned, the Sunday comics were the whole reason for newspapers to exist. On weekdays, I read only the strips I liked; but on Sundays, I read them all, and often several times. The Sunday comics were always the most fun to look at, so when I finally got the chance to draw my own comic strip, I knew I wanted to make the Sunday *Calvin and Hobbes* something special.

It took me a little while to learn to use the larger Sunday space effectively. It requires a somewhat different pace for the humor, and, of course, a big color panel is no place to find out that you don't know how to draw the back of your character's head. The Sunday strip shows off both strengths and weaknesses.

Occasionally I would see that an idea I'd written for a Sunday strip was not as substantial as I'd hoped it would be, and I'd realize that some of the panels and dialogue weren't adding anything significant to the story. If that were the case, I'd remove everything extraneous and use the trimmed idea for a daily strip instead. I held the Sundays to a different standard: any idea for the Sunday strip had to need the extra space. I felt a Sunday strip should do something that was impossible the rest of the week.

Over the years, I learned that daily strips are better suited for certain kinds of ideas, while Sunday strips are better for others. The daily strip is quick and to the point, perfect for a simple observation, or a short exchange between characters. Daily strips are also better for long stories, where a certain suspense can be fostered by continuing the story day after day, and the reader can remember what happened previously.

Extended conversations with real back and forth dialogue, however, don't work very well in four tiny panels—the dialogue balloons crowd out the drawings and the strip loses its grace. In a Sunday strip, you can spread out, and let the characters yap a bit. This is often funny in itself, and it's a wonderful way to let the characters' personalities emerge. It also lets you explore a topic a bit more fully.

You can talk about things without reducing them to one-liners right away.

And, of course, in today's minuscule comics, if an idea requires any real drawing, the Sunday strip is the only possible place for it. Likewise, any complex storytelling problem—a strip illustrating a long expanse of time, for example, or an event depicted in a succession of very tiny moments—is futile in the daily format. Calvin's fantasies generally migrated to the Sunday page for this reason.

In short, the Sunday page offered unique opportunities, and I deliberately tried to come up with ideas that could take advantage of them.

I usually wrote the Sunday strips separately from the dailies. For the daily strips, I tried to write an entire month's worth of ideas before inking any of them. This allowed a long period for editing and rewriting. I was less able to do this for the Sunday strips because the Sundays need to be drawn weeks further in advance and because the strips took so much longer to draw. If at all possible, however, I would try to keep two or three Sunday ideas ahead of the deadlines. I always wanted to reserve the option of abandoning an idea that didn't stand up to a few weeks of scrutiny.

For those who are interested in technical matters, the early strips were drawn on any cheap pad of Bristol board the local art supply store happened to stock. The paper was usually rather thin and sometimes the sheet wouldn't accept the ink consistently (bad sizing or something), which would make drawing aggravating and time consuming. Eventually I switched to heavier Strathmore Bristol board, which was much nicer. I used a 2H pencil to rough in the drawing, and then inked with a small sable brush and India ink. I did as little pencil work as possible in order to keep the inking more spontaneous, although the more elaborate panels required more preliminary drawing. For lettering, I used a Rapidograph cartridge pen. I drew the dialogue balloons and a few odds and ends with a crow quill pen. To cover up unwanted marks, I used various brands of Wite-Out, and in the early days, typewriter correction fluid. (Remember typewriters?) No doubt this stuff will eat through the paper or turn green in a few years, but as the original cartoons were intended for reproduction, not picture frames and gallery walls, I did not overly concern myself with archival issues or, for that matter, neatness. At some point along the way, however, I did ask the syndicate to send the printers a quality reproduction of the Sunday cartoon, rather than the original drawing, in order to reduce the amount of tape, registration marks, and general crunchings and manglings to which the drawings had previously been subjected.

Coloring the strips was a slow and tedious process. My syndicate gave me a printed sheet showing

numbered squares of color, each a mixture of various percentages of red, yellow, and blue. Using this sheet as a guide, I taped some tracing paper over the finished cartoon, and painted watercolor approximations of the available colors in the areas I wanted. This would give me a very rough idea of what the newspaper version might look like. Then I numbered each little spot of color. As the Sunday strips became more visually complex, and as I started to use color more deliberately for effects, this process became a real chore. These days, I believe much of it can be done with a few clicks of a mouse.

Colors take on different characteristics when placed next to other colors (a neutral-seeming gray might look greenish and dark next to one color, but brownish and pale in relation to another). Because of this, I came up with one little trick for coloring the strip. I cut out each of the color squares provided by the printer, so I had a stack of colors (like paint chips), rather than a sheet. By laying out the cut squares and physically placing one color next to the others I expected to use, I could see exactly how each color behaved in that particular context. As I got better at this, I was able to choose appropriate "palettes" for each strip, and create moods with color. One strip might call for contrasting, bright colors; another strip might be done with a limited group of soft, warm colors; another idea might call for a close range of grays and darks, and so on. If I made Calvin's skin a dull pink-gray to suggest dim lighting at night, I would have to find a dull yellow-gray that would suggest his hair in the same light. These challenges took an inordinate amount of time for work on deadline, but I was often quite proud of the results. A comic strip should always be fun to look at, and good use of color can contribute to that appeal. More than that, color creates its own emotional impact, which can make the drawing more expressive.

The half-page Sunday format required certain guaranteed panel divisions. The strip had to be drawn in three rows of equal height, and there was one unmovable panel division within each row. This allowed editors to reduce and reconfigure the strip to suit their particular space needs. The same strip could run in several shapes by restacking the panels.

Editors commonly removed the entire top row altogether, so in essence, a third of the strip had to be wasted on "throwaway panels" that many readers would never see. The fixed panel divisions were also annoying because they limited my ability to compose the strip to best suit the idea. For example, they often forced a small panel where I needed more space for words.

Of course, a big part of cartooning is learning to work effectively within tight space constraints. Much of cartooning's power comes from its ability to do more with less: when the drawings and ideas are

distilled to their essences, the result can be more beautiful and powerful for having eliminated the clutter. That said, there is a point at which simplification thwarts good storytelling. You can't condense *Moby Dick* into a paragraph and get the same effect. Over the years, my frustration increased and I became convinced that I could draw a better comic strip than the current newspaper format was permitting. Looking at examples of comics from the 1930s, when a Sunday strip could fill an entire page, I was amazed by the long-forgotten possibilities out there.

I took a sabbatical after resolving a long and emotionally draining fight to prevent *Calvin and Hobbes* from being merchandised. Looking for a way to rekindle my enthusiasm for the duration of a new contract term, I proposed a redesigned Sunday format that would permit more panel flexibility. To my surprise and delight, Universal responded with an offer to market the strip as an unbreakable half page (more space than I'd dared to ask for), despite the expected resistance of editors.

To this day, my syndicate assures me that some editors liked the new format, appreciated the difference, and were happy to run the larger strip, but I think it's fair to say that this was not the most common reaction. The syndicate had warned me to prepare for numerous cancellations of the Sunday feature, but after a few weeks of dealing with howling, purple-faced editors, the syndicate suggested that papers could reduce the strip to the size tabloid newspapers used for their smaller sheets of paper. Another strip could then run vertically down the side. Consequently, while some papers, primarily in larger markets, ran the strip as a half page, other papers reduced it. In some of the latter papers (including the one I read at the time), I actually lost ground: the new Sunday strip was printed even smaller than before. I was in no mood to take on new fights, so I focused on the bright side: I had complete freedom of design and there were virtually no cancellations.

For all the yelling and screaming by outraged editors, I remain convinced that the larger Sunday strip gave newspapers a better product and made the comics section more fun for readers. Comics are a visual medium. A strip with a lot of drawing can be exciting and add some variety. Proud as I am that I was able to draw a larger strip, I don't expect to see it happen again any time soon. In the newspaper business, space is money, and I suspect most editors would still say that the difference is not worth the cost. Sadly, the situation is a vicious circle: because there's no room for better artwork, the comics are simply drawn; because they're simply drawn, why should they have more room?

Business controversies aside, the new format opened up new ways to tell stories, and I drew different

kinds of strips as a result. I could write and draw the strip exactly as I imagined it, so it truly challenged my abilities. Whereas Sunday strips had previously taken me a full day to draw and color, a complex strip would now take me well into a second day to finish. Deadlines discourage this kind of indulgence, and I had to steal that extra time from what would have been some semblance of an ordinary life, but I was thrilled to expand the strip's world.

Laying out the panels became a job in itself, now that I was no longer confined to horizontal rows. I could place boxes anywhere and any size, but the reader's eye needs to flow naturally to the proper panels without confusion, and big panels need to be designed in such a way that they don't divert attention and spoil surprises. The graphic needs of each panel must be accommodated and the panels themselves should form a pleasing arrangement so the entire page is attractive, balanced, and unified as well. Here again I looked for guidance in the gorgeous Sunday pages of George Herriman's *Krazy Kat*.

The new Sunday format necessitated a change in the format of my book collections as well. Having won a bigger strip in newspapers, I wanted the book reproductions to reflect the strip's new impact as much as possible by printing the Sunday strips large. This resulted in the rather awkward horizontal format of my later books. They stick out of bookshelves, but the strips look nice. From this point on, the Sunday strips were reproduced in color with each collection, not just in the "treasury" collections, as before. (Here's a piece of trivia: because of the timing of the book format change, the cartoons from the *Snow Goons* collection were never put in a treasury book, so those Sunday strips have been reprinted only in black-and-white.)

Ten years after starting *Calvin and Hobbes*, I ended the strip. As much as I knew I'd miss the characters, the decision was long anticipated on my part. Professionally, I had accomplished far more than I'd ever set out to do and there were no more mountains I wanted to climb. Creatively, my interests were shifting away from cartooning toward painting, where I could develop my drawing skills further. And personally, I wanted to restore some balance to my life. I had given the strip all my time and energy for a decade (and was happy to do so), but now I was that much older and I wanted to work at a more thoughtful pace, out of the limelight, and without the pressures and restrictions of newspapers.

The final *Calvin and Hobbes* strip was a Sunday strip. The deadline for Sunday strips being early, I drew it well before writing the daily strips that would eventually precede it in the newspaper. I very much wanted to hit the right note for this final strip. I think it worked, but it was a bittersweet strip to draw.

Since *Calvin and Hobbes*, I've been teaching myself how to paint, and trying to learn something about music. I have no background in either subject, and there are certainly days when I wonder what made me trade proficiency and understanding in one field for clumsiness and ignorance in these others. On better days, I enjoy having so many new challenges and surprises. Even so, these new endeavors have only deepened my appreciation for comics. I no longer take quite so much for granted the versatility of comics and their ability to depict complex ideas in a beautiful, accessible, and entertaining form. For all their seeming simplicity, the expressive possibilities of comics rival those of any other art form. Five years after *Calvin and Hobbes*, I love the comics as much as ever.

Bill Watterson
Summer 2001

CALVIN AND HOBBES
SUNDAY PAGES 1985-1995

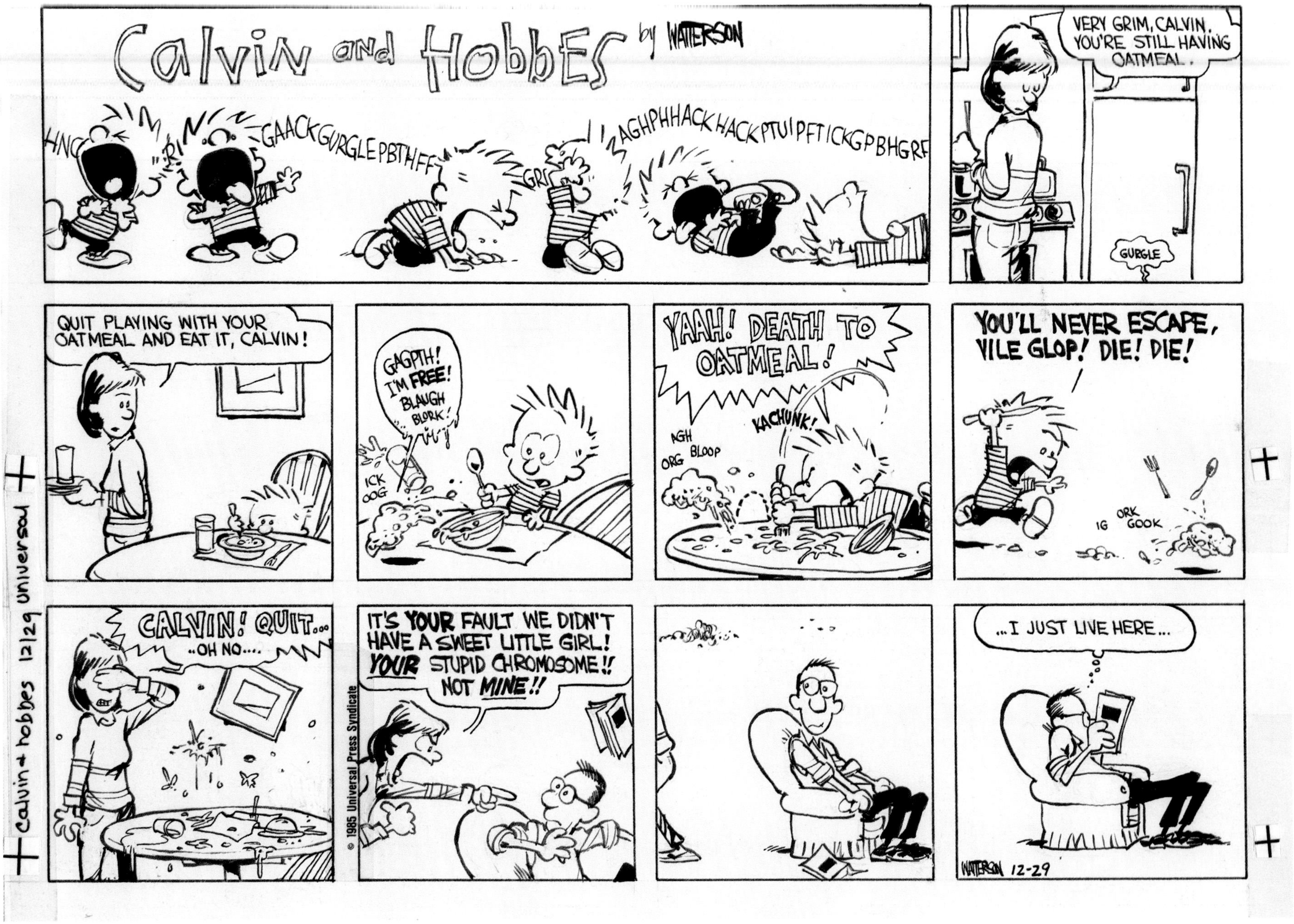
Calvin and Hobbes by WATTERSON
HNG
RI
GAACKGURGLEPBTHFF
GRI
AGHPHHACK HACK PTUI PFTICKGPBHGRF
VERY GRIM, CALVIN. YOU'RE STILL HAVING OATMEAL.
GURGLE
QUIT PLAYING WITH YOUR OATMEAL AND EAT IT, CALVIN!
GAGPTH! I'M FREE! BLAUGH BLORK!
ICK OOG
YAAH! DEATH TO OATMEAL!
KACHUNK!
NGH ORG BLOOP
YOU'LL NEVER ESCAPE, VILE GLOP! DIE! DIE!
IG ORK GOOK
CALVIN! QUIT...
..OH NO....
IT'S YOUR FAULT WE DIDN'T HAVE A SWEET LITTLE GIRL! YOUR STUPID CHROMOSOME!! NOT MINE!!
...I JUST LIVE HERE...
WATTERSON 12-29
© 1985 Universal Press Syndicate
Calvin + hobbes 12/29 universal

DECEMBER 29, 1985

I drew this about a month into the strip, when *Calvin and Hobbes* appeared in a few dozen newspapers. My own newspaper didn't carry the strip, which made my job feel very abstract.

The first two panels, composing the entire top row, are the "throwaway" panels that many newspapers would eliminate to make the strip smaller. Knowing that few readers would see it, I often wasted most of the space up there, but here I've drawn a nice little series of Calvin carrying on. The lower panels are all the same size. This was not an

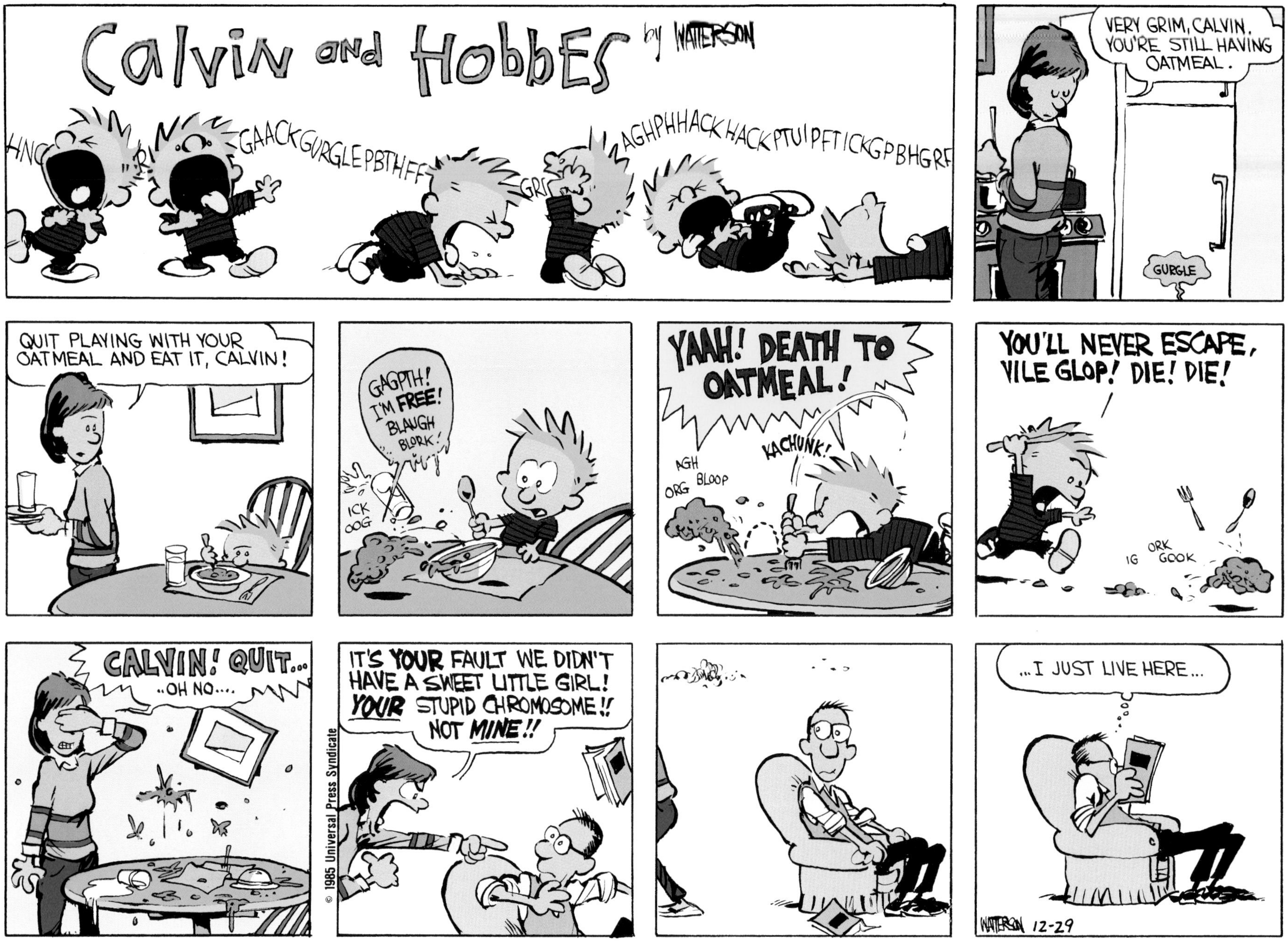
Calvin and Hobbes by WATTERSON
HNG
GAACKGURGLEPBTHFF
AGHPHHACK HACK PTUI PFT ICKGPBHGRF
VERY GRIM, CALVIN. YOU'RE STILL HAVING OATMEAL.
GURGLE
QUIT PLAYING WITH YOUR OATMEAL AND EAT IT, CALVIN!
GAGPTH! I'M FREE! BLAUGH BLORK!
ICK OOG
YAAH! DEATH TO OATMEAL!
KACHUNK!
AGH ORG BLOOP
YOU'LL NEVER ESCAPE, VILE GLOP! DIE! DIE!
IG ORK GOOK
CALVIN! QUIT... ..OH NO....
IT'S YOUR FAULT WE DIDN'T HAVE A SWEET LITTLE GIRL! YOUR STUPID CHROMOSOME!! NOT MINE!!
© 1985 Universal Press Syndicate
...I JUST LIVE HERE...
WATTERSON 12-29

aesthetic decision; I really didn't know what else to do. Fortunately, lack of drawing ability is rarely a liability in cartooning, and this arrangement, while unimaginative, is nevertheless effective in its simplicity and clarity. Also notice that, in a single strip, we learn something about the personality of all three characters. From the beginning, *Calvin and Hobbes* was more about characters than jokes, and I think this was an important reason the strip was able to attract an audience and survive the tough first years.

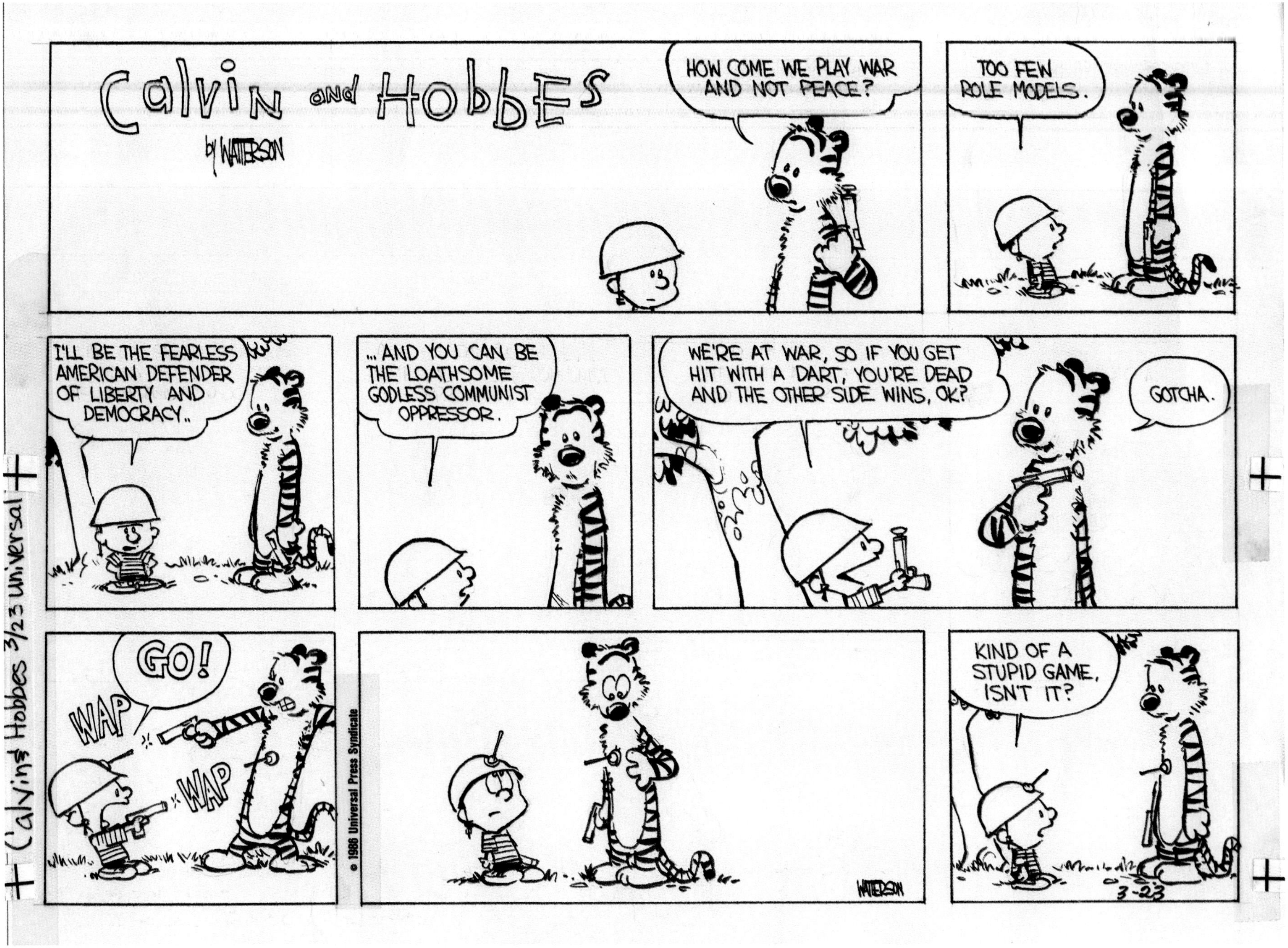
Calvin and HOBBES
by WATTERSON
HOW COME WE PLAY WAR AND NOT PEACE?
TOO FEW ROLE MODELS.
I'LL BE THE FEARLESS AMERICAN DEFENDER OF LIBERTY AND DEMOCRACY..
...AND YOU CAN BE THE LOATHSOME GODLESS COMMUNIST OPPRESSOR.
WE'RE AT WAR, SO IF YOU GET HIT WITH A DART, YOU'RE DEAD AND THE OTHER SIDE WINS, OK?
GOTCHA.
GO!
WAP
WAP
© 1986 Universal Press Syndicate
WATTERSON
KIND OF A STUPID GAME, ISN'T IT?
3-23
Calvin and Hobbes 3/23 Universal

MARCH 23, 1986

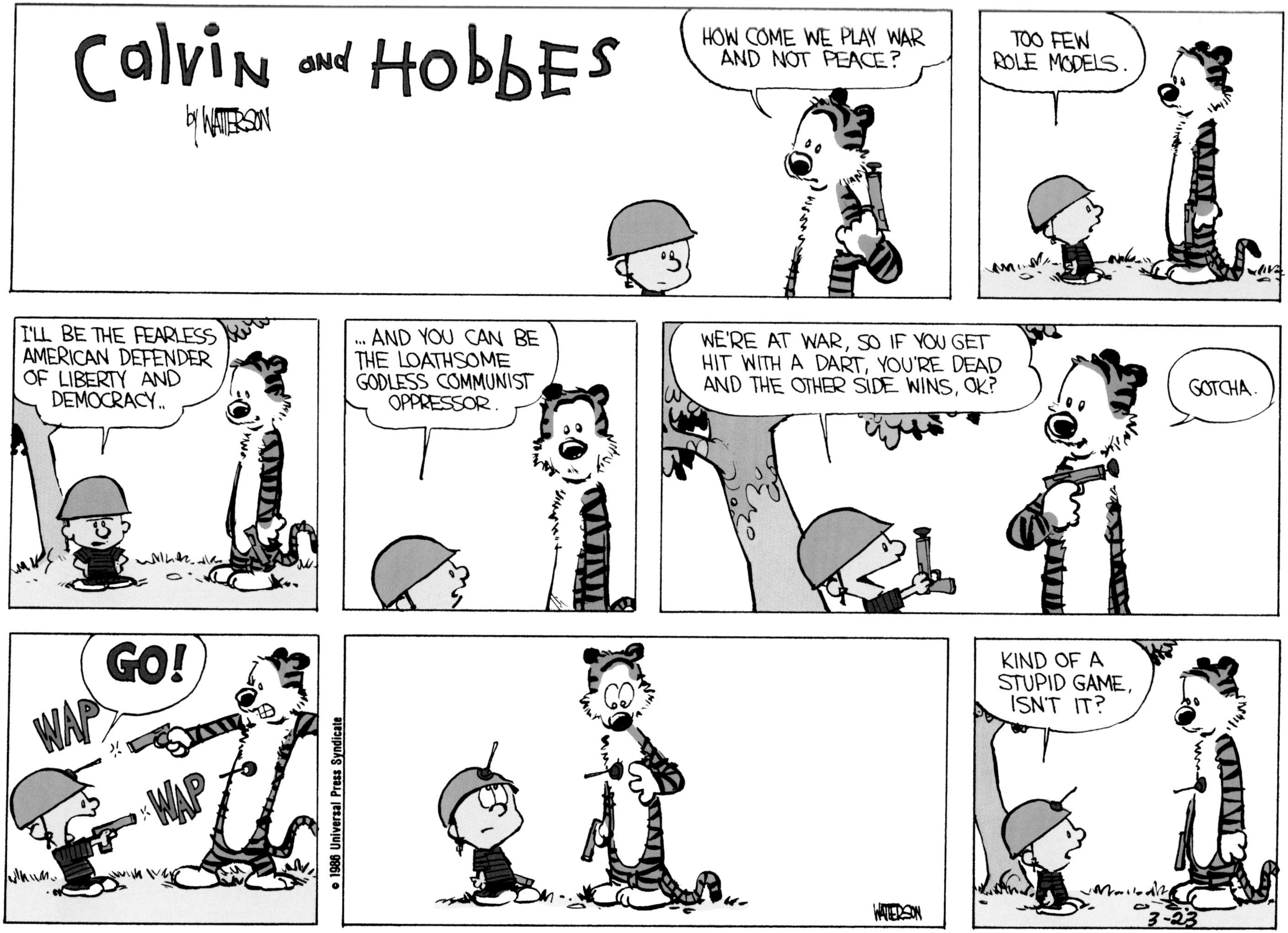
Calvin and Hobbes
by WATTERSON
HOW COME WE PLAY WAR AND NOT PEACE?
TOO FEW ROLE MODELS.
I'LL BE THE FEARLESS AMERICAN DEFENDER OF LIBERTY AND DEMOCRACY..
... AND YOU CAN BE THE LOATHSOME GODLESS COMMUNIST OPPRESSOR.
WE'RE AT WAR, SO IF YOU GET HIT WITH A DART, YOU'RE DEAD AND THE OTHER SIDE WINS, OK?
GOTCHA.
GO!
WAP
WAP
© 1986 Universal Press Syndicate
WATTERSON
KIND OF A STUPID GAME, ISN'T IT?
3-23

This was drawn when President Reagan was staring down the Soviet Union with an arms buildup. It all seems very long ago now ... thank heavens.

On the original drawing, you can see that the word "okay" has been whited out and changed to "OK," making the little bulge at the end of the balloon unnecessary. The syndicate apparently felt that OK was more correct than okay. Eventually I learned to write it that way myself and save the syndicate some trouble.

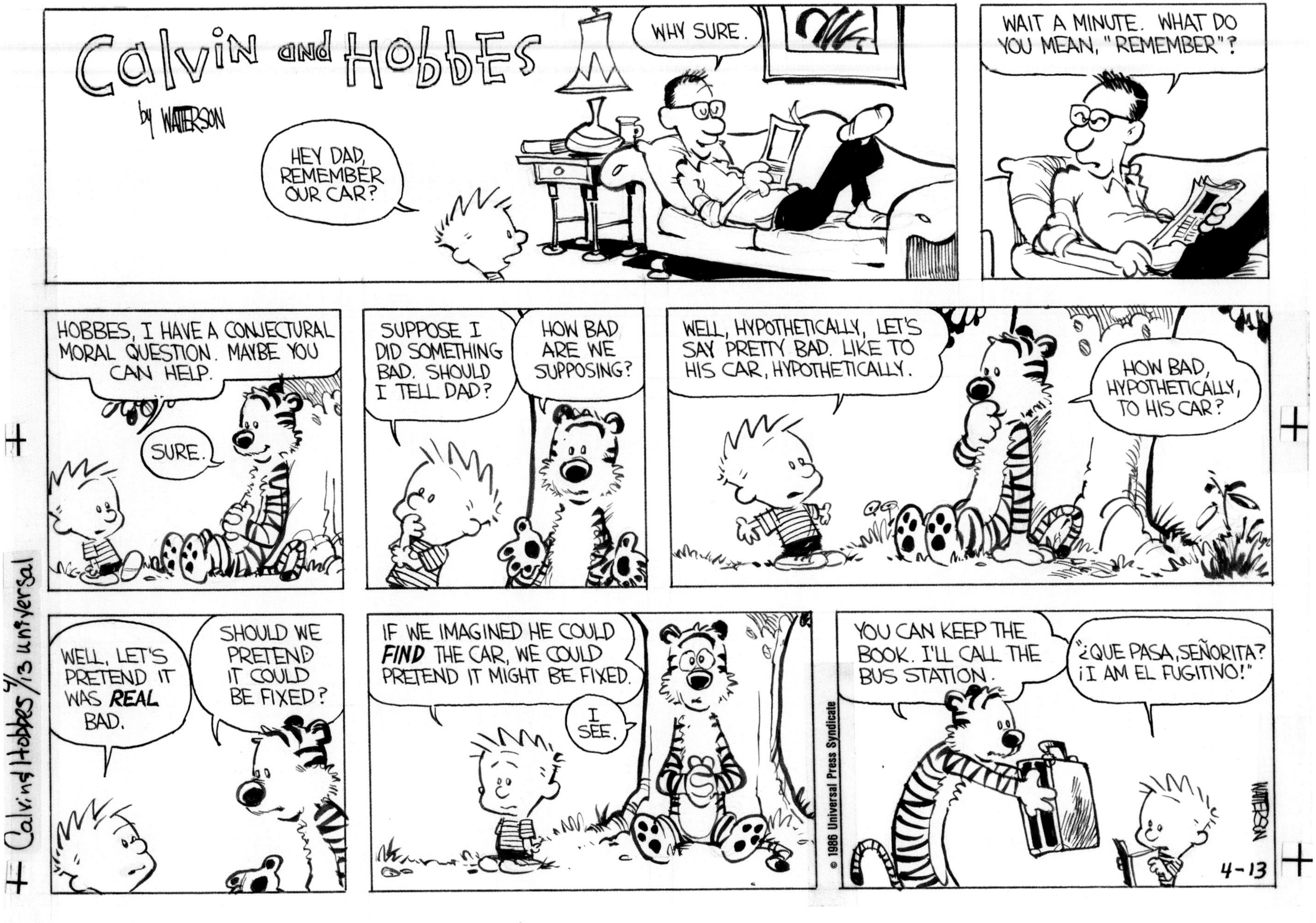
Calvin and Hobbes
by WATTERSON
HEY DAD, REMEMBER OUR CAR?
WHY SURE.
WAIT A MINUTE. WHAT DO YOU MEAN, "REMEMBER"?
HOBBES, I HAVE A CONJECTURAL MORAL QUESTION. MAYBE YOU CAN HELP.
SURE.
SUPPOSE I DID SOMETHING BAD. SHOULD I TELL DAD?
HOW BAD ARE WE SUPPOSING?
WELL, HYPOTHETICALLY, LET'S SAY PRETTY BAD. LIKE TO HIS CAR, HYPOTHETICALLY.
HOW BAD, HYPOTHETICALLY, TO HIS CAR?
WELL, LET'S PRETEND IT WAS REAL BAD.
SHOULD WE PRETEND IT COULD BE FIXED?
IF WE IMAGINED HE COULD FIND THE CAR, WE COULD PRETEND IT MIGHT BE FIXED.
I SEE.
YOU CAN KEEP THE BOOK. I'LL CALL THE BUS STATION.
"¿QUE PASA, SEÑORITA? ¡I AM EL FUGITIVO!"
© 1986 Universal Press Syndicate
WATTERSON
4-13
Calvin and Hobbes 4/13 universal

April 13, 1986

Note the pads on Hobbes's hands. I liked those as reminders that his hands were really paws, but I soon decided that the black circles were visually disruptive, and prevented the hands from being read and understood instantly. The pads stayed on Hobbes's feet, but hands are too expressive to clutter up.

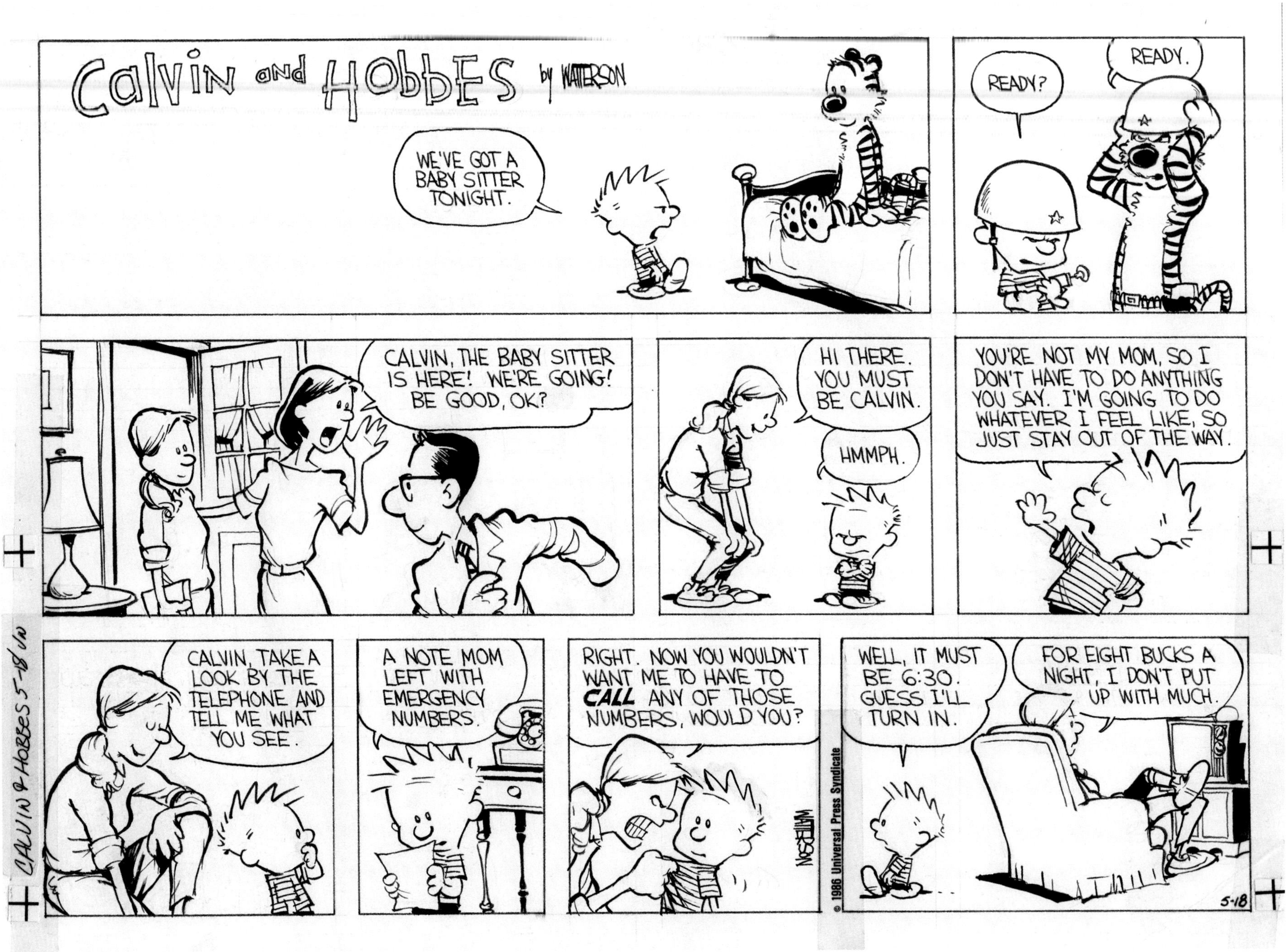
Calvin and Hobbes by WATTERSON
WE'VE GOT A BABY SITTER TONIGHT.
READY?
READY.
CALVIN, THE BABY SITTER IS HERE! WE'RE GOING! BE GOOD, OK?
HI THERE. YOU MUST BE CALVIN.
HMMPH.
YOU'RE NOT MY MOM, SO I DON'T HAVE TO DO ANYTHING YOU SAY. I'M GOING TO DO WHATEVER I FEEL LIKE, SO JUST STAY OUT OF THE WAY.
CALVIN, TAKE A LOOK BY THE TELEPHONE AND TELL ME WHAT YOU SEE.
A NOTE MOM LEFT WITH EMERGENCY NUMBERS.
RIGHT. NOW YOU WOULDN'T WANT ME TO HAVE TO CALL ANY OF THOSE NUMBERS, WOULD YOU?
WATTERSON
© 1986 Universal Press Syndicate
WELL, IT MUST BE 6:30. GUESS I'LL TURN IN.
FOR EIGHT BUCKS A NIGHT, I DON'T PUT UP WITH MUCH.
5-18
CALVIN & HOBBES 5-18 UW

MAY 18, 1986

This was the introduction of Calvin's babysitter, Roz. She doesn't even have a name here, as I never expected to use her again. Her ferocious personality surprised me though, so she came back several times.

At that point, I used her for longer stories, continuing across daily strips, where the conflicts could play out on a larger scale.

Notice the rotary telephone and the television with UHF and VHF channel knobs. These were outdated even in 1986, but I think they're funnier looking, and have more personality, than the new ones. I think my parents were the last people in America to watch a black-and-white TV, so old appliances fit the strip that way, too.

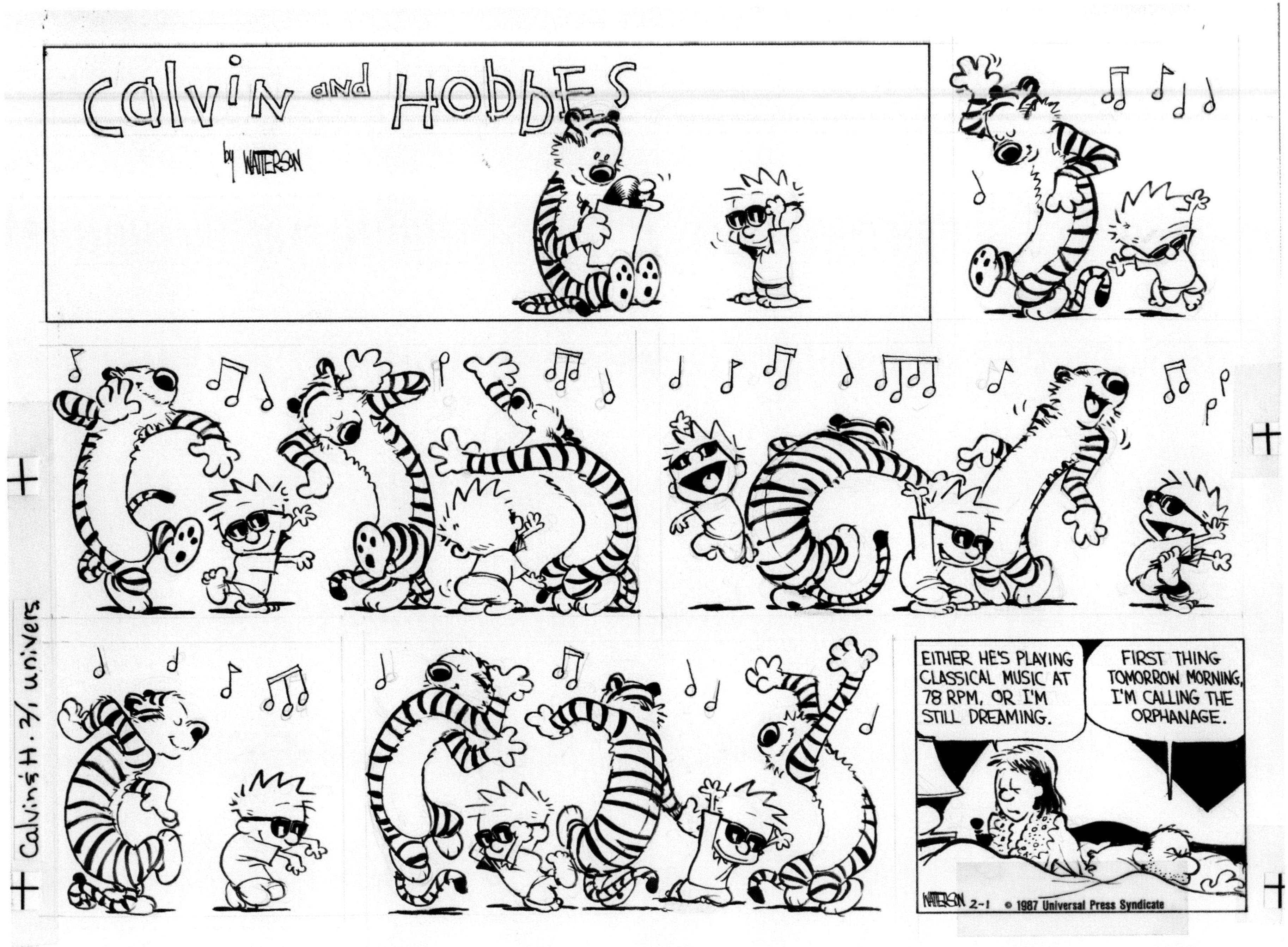
Calvin and HOBBES
by WATTERSON
EITHER HE'S PLAYING CLASSICAL MUSIC AT 78 RPM, OR I'M STILL DREAMING.
FIRST THING TOMORROW MORNING, I'M CALLING THE ORPHANAGE.
WATTERSON 2-1 © 1987 Universal Press Syndicate

FEBRUARY 1, 1987

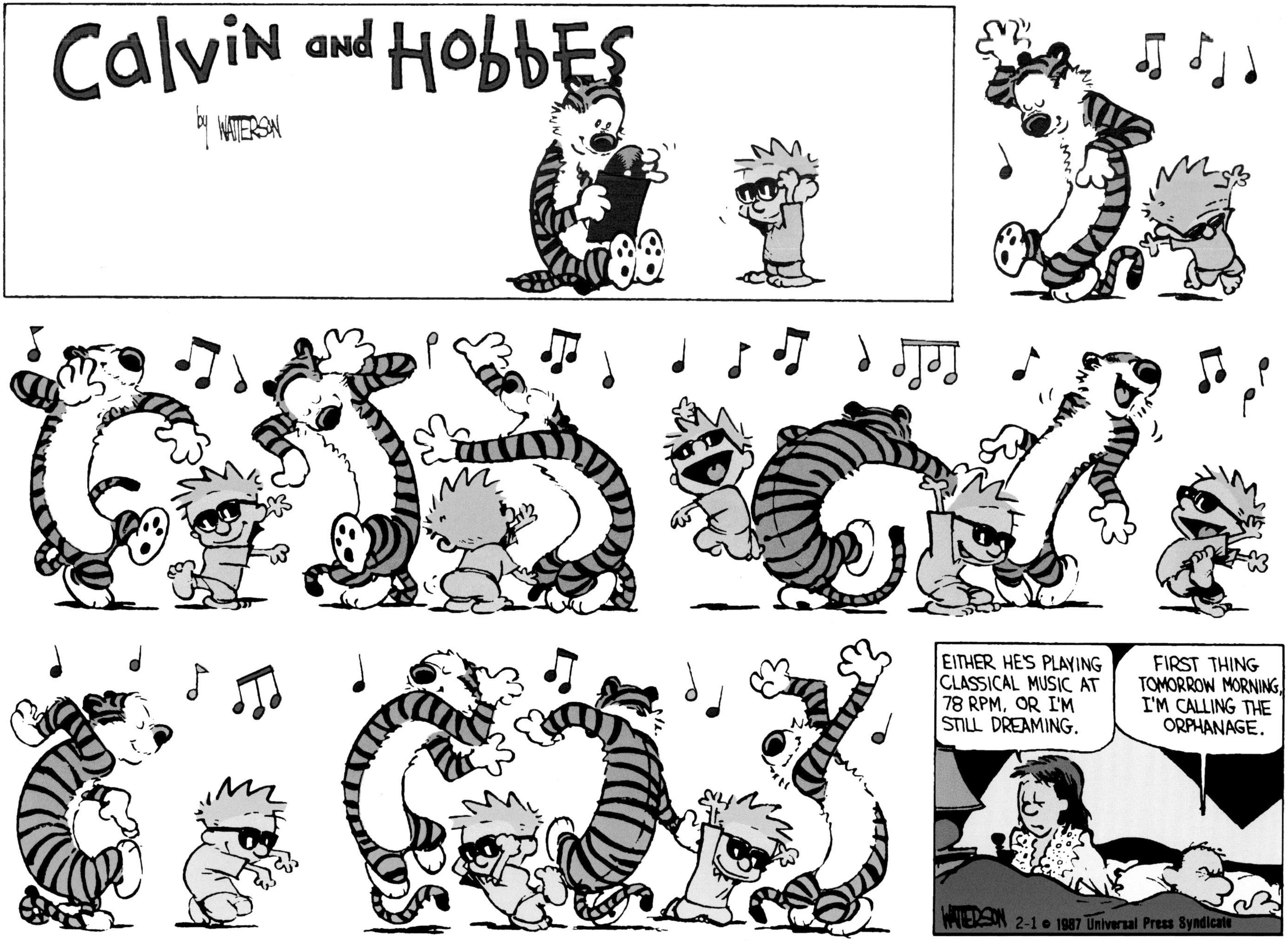
Calvin and Hobbes
by WATTERSON
EITHER HE'S PLAYING CLASSICAL MUSIC AT 78 RPM, OR I'M STILL DREAMING.
FIRST THING TOMORROW MORNING, I'M CALLING THE ORPHANAGE.
WATTERSON 2-1 © 1987 Universal Press Syndicate

Calvin and Hobbes doesn't seem that long ago, but here we are with an LP in the first panel. The drawings from this strip were often ripped off for illegal T-shirts and the like.

I wanted a page of drawings that flowed into each other, but you can see the gaps (in the middle of the second row and at left in the third row) where panel divisions were mandated. By this time, the characters were becoming more physically three-dimensional in my mind, and I had fun animating them.

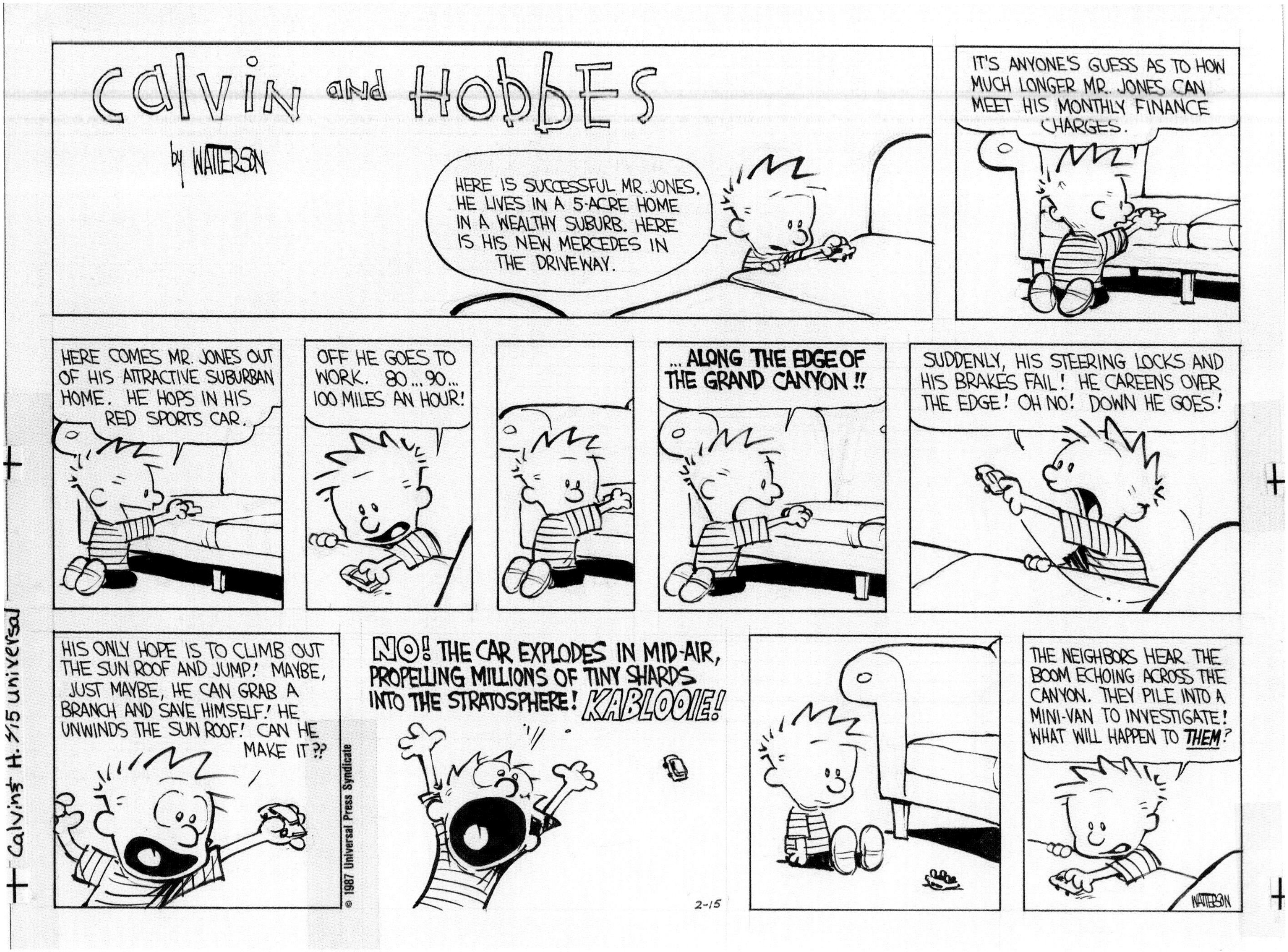
Calvin and HobbES
by WATTERSON
HERE IS SUCCESSFUL MR. JONES. HE LIVES IN A 5-ACRE HOME IN A WEALTHY SUBURB. HERE IS HIS NEW MERCEDES IN THE DRIVEWAY.
IT'S ANYONE'S GUESS AS TO HOW MUCH LONGER MR. JONES CAN MEET HIS MONTHLY FINANCE CHARGES.
HERE COMES MR. JONES OUT OF HIS ATTRACTIVE SUBURBAN HOME. HE HOPS IN HIS RED SPORTS CAR.
OFF HE GOES TO WORK. 80...90... 100 MILES AN HOUR!
...ALONG THE EDGE OF THE GRAND CANYON!!
SUDDENLY, HIS STEERING LOCKS AND HIS BRAKES FAIL! HE CAREENS OVER THE EDGE! OH NO! DOWN HE GOES!
HIS ONLY HOPE IS TO CLIMB OUT THE SUN ROOF AND JUMP! MAYBE, JUST MAYBE, HE CAN GRAB A BRANCH AND SAVE HIMSELF! HE UNWINDS THE SUN ROOF! CAN HE MAKE IT??
NO! THE CAR EXPLODES IN MID-AIR, PROPELLING MILLIONS OF TINY SHARDS INTO THE STRATOSPHERE! KABLOOIE!
THE NEIGHBORS HEAR THE BOOM ECHOING ACROSS THE CANYON. THEY PILE INTO A MINI-VAN TO INVESTIGATE! WHAT WILL HAPPEN TO THEM?
WATTERSON
© 1987 Universal Press Syndicate
2-15
Calvin+ H. 2/15 universal

FEBRUARY 15, 1987

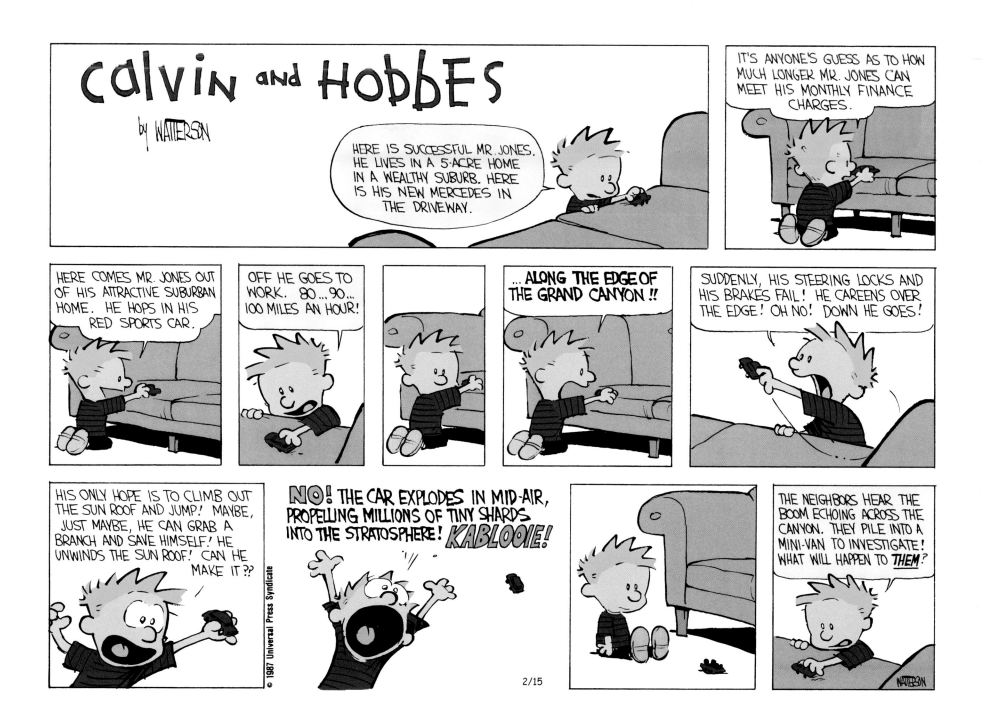

This is one of the rare Sunday strips where the pictures don't do much of the work. A purely verbal strip is tolerable once in a while for variety, but boy, the writing had better be working hard.

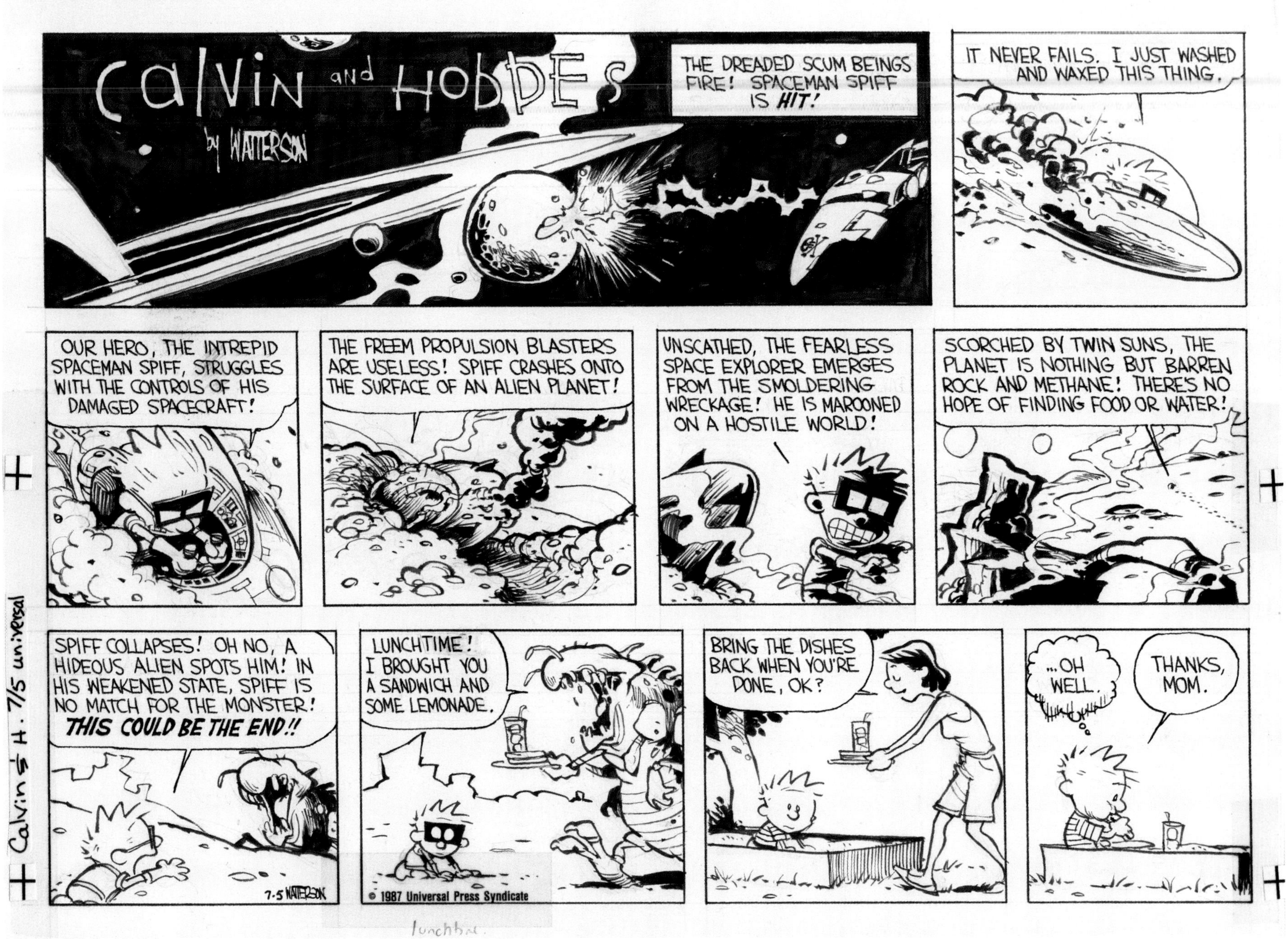
Calvin and Hobbes
by WATTERSON
THE DREADED SCUM BEINGS FIRE! SPACEMAN SPIFF IS HIT!
IT NEVER FAILS. I JUST WASHED AND WAXED THIS THING.
OUR HERO, THE INTREPID SPACEMAN SPIFF, STRUGGLES WITH THE CONTROLS OF HIS DAMAGED SPACECRAFT!
THE FREEM PROPULSION BLASTERS ARE USELESS! SPIFF CRASHES ONTO THE SURFACE OF AN ALIEN PLANET!
UNSCATHED, THE FEARLESS SPACE EXPLORER EMERGES FROM THE SMOLDERING WRECKAGE! HE IS MAROONED ON A HOSTILE WORLD!
SCORCHED BY TWIN SUNS, THE PLANET IS NOTHING BUT BARREN ROCK AND METHANE! THERE'S NO HOPE OF FINDING FOOD OR WATER!
SPIFF COLLAPSES! OH NO, A HIDEOUS ALIEN SPOTS HIM! IN HIS WEAKENED STATE, SPIFF IS NO MATCH FOR THE MONSTER! THIS COULD BE THE END!!
7-5 WATTERSON
LUNCHTIME! I BROUGHT YOU A SANDWICH AND SOME LEMONADE.
© 1987 Universal Press Syndicate
BRING THE DISHES BACK WHEN YOU'RE DONE, OK?
...OH WELL.
THANKS, MOM.

JULY 5, 1987

The Spaceman Spiff episodes were always fun to draw. I never really took the stories anywhere, but I loved drawing the landscapes, monsters, and spaceships. The landscape here is invented and rather generic, but in later strips, southern Utah became a great inspiration. The long throwaway panel at the top shows the type of scale and atmosphere one can evoke with a bit more room. Remove it, as many papers did, and the strip looks much more static and restrained.

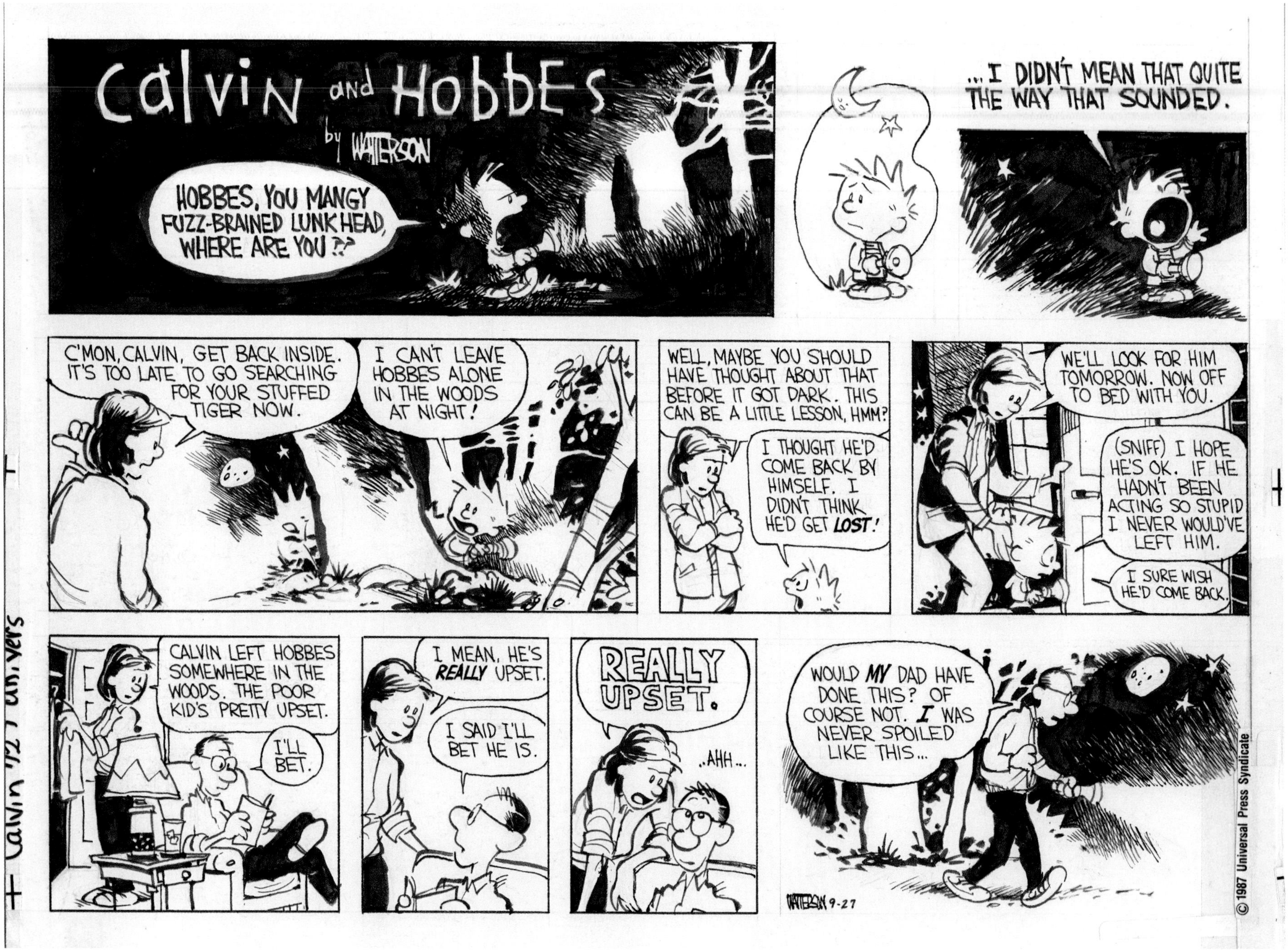
Calvin and Hobbes
by WATTERSON
HOBBES, YOU MANGY FUZZ-BRAINED LUNKHEAD, WHERE ARE YOU ??
...I DIDN'T MEAN THAT QUITE THE WAY THAT SOUNDED.
C'MON, CALVIN, GET BACK INSIDE. IT'S TOO LATE TO GO SEARCHING FOR YOUR STUFFED TIGER NOW.
I CAN'T LEAVE HOBBES ALONE IN THE WOODS AT NIGHT!
WELL, MAYBE YOU SHOULD HAVE THOUGHT ABOUT THAT BEFORE IT GOT DARK. THIS CAN BE A LITTLE LESSON, HMM?
I THOUGHT HE'D COME BACK BY HIMSELF. I DIDN'T THINK HE'D GET LOST!
WE'LL LOOK FOR HIM TOMORROW. NOW OFF TO BED WITH YOU.
(SNIFF) I HOPE HE'S OK. IF HE HADN'T BEEN ACTING SO STUPID I NEVER WOULD'VE LEFT HIM.
I SURE WISH HE'D COME BACK.
CALVIN LEFT HOBBES SOMEWHERE IN THE WOODS. THE POOR KID'S PRETTY UPSET.
I'LL BET.
I MEAN, HE'S REALLY UPSET.
I SAID I'LL BET HE IS.
REALLY UPSET.
..AHH...
WOULD MY DAD HAVE DONE THIS? OF COURSE NOT. I WAS NEVER SPOILED LIKE THIS...
WATTERSON 9-27
© 1987 Universal Press Syndicate

September 27, 1987

This strip was part of a story that was continuing across the daily strips. The daily strips were sold separately from the Sunday strips, and newspapers did not always buy both. Consequently, readers might be seeing the whole story, all of the story except this strip, or this strip and none of the story. Thus, the challenge for me was to make this strip integral to the plot, yet entirely self-sufficient, yet utterly expendable. I believe I succeeded, although I'm hard-pressed to say why I bothered.

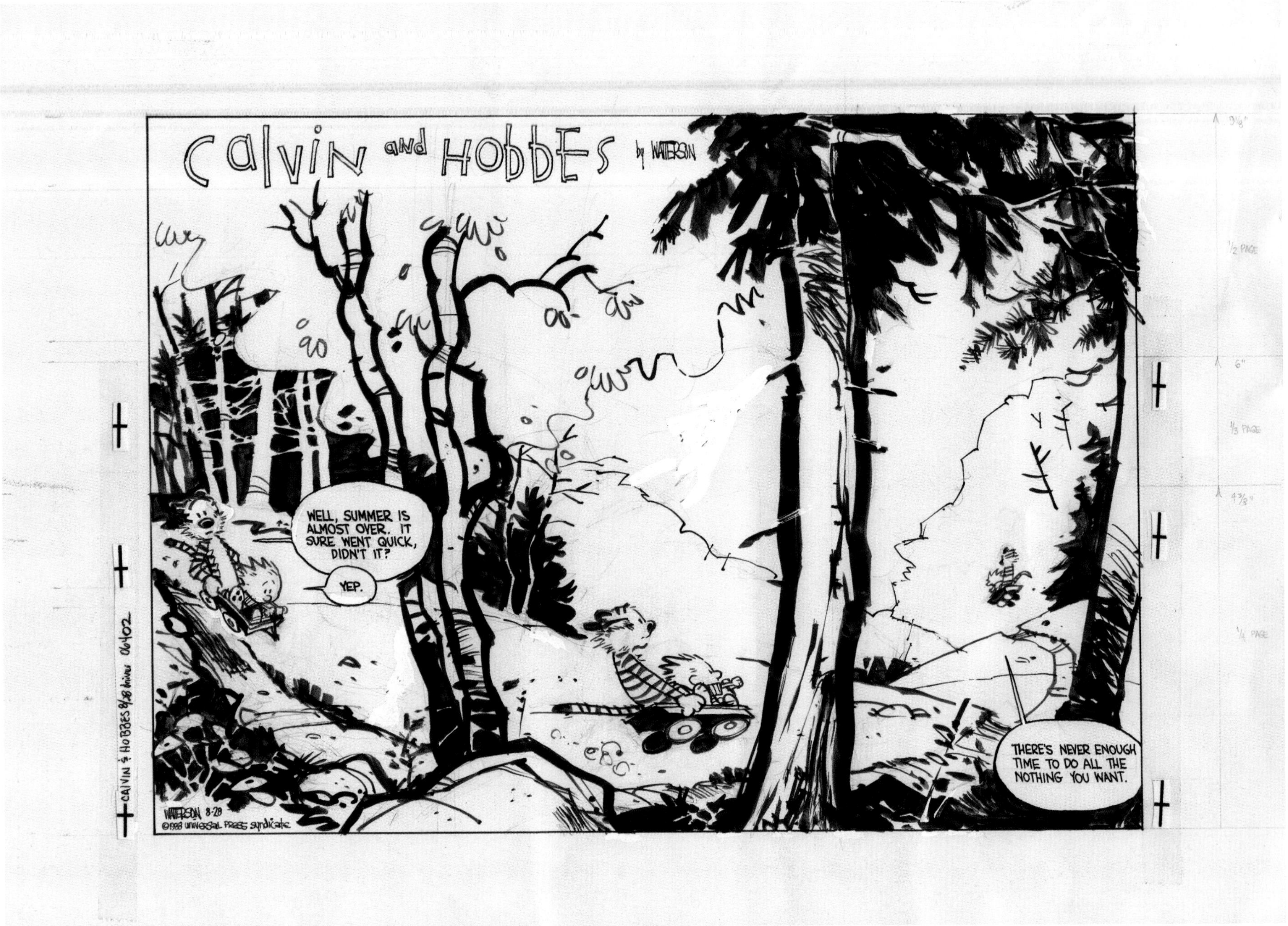
Calvin and HOBBES by WATTERSON
WELL, SUMMER IS ALMOST OVER. IT SURE WENT QUICK, DIDN'T IT?
YEP.
THERE'S NEVER ENOUGH TIME TO DO ALL THE NOTHING YOU WANT.
WATTERSON 8-28
©1988 Universal Press Syndicate
1/2 PAGE
1/3 PAGE
1/4 PAGE

AUGUST 28, 1988

I liked the idea in this strip enough to put it in a Sunday strip, but it's very simple and I didn't want to pad it with the number of panels the usual format required. To draw the strip as one large panel, I had to condense all the words and action at the very bottom, so editors could hack away at the rest of the drawing if they wanted to print a smaller strip. On the edge of the original, you can see where I've marked the various page divisions. As is, the strip would run as a

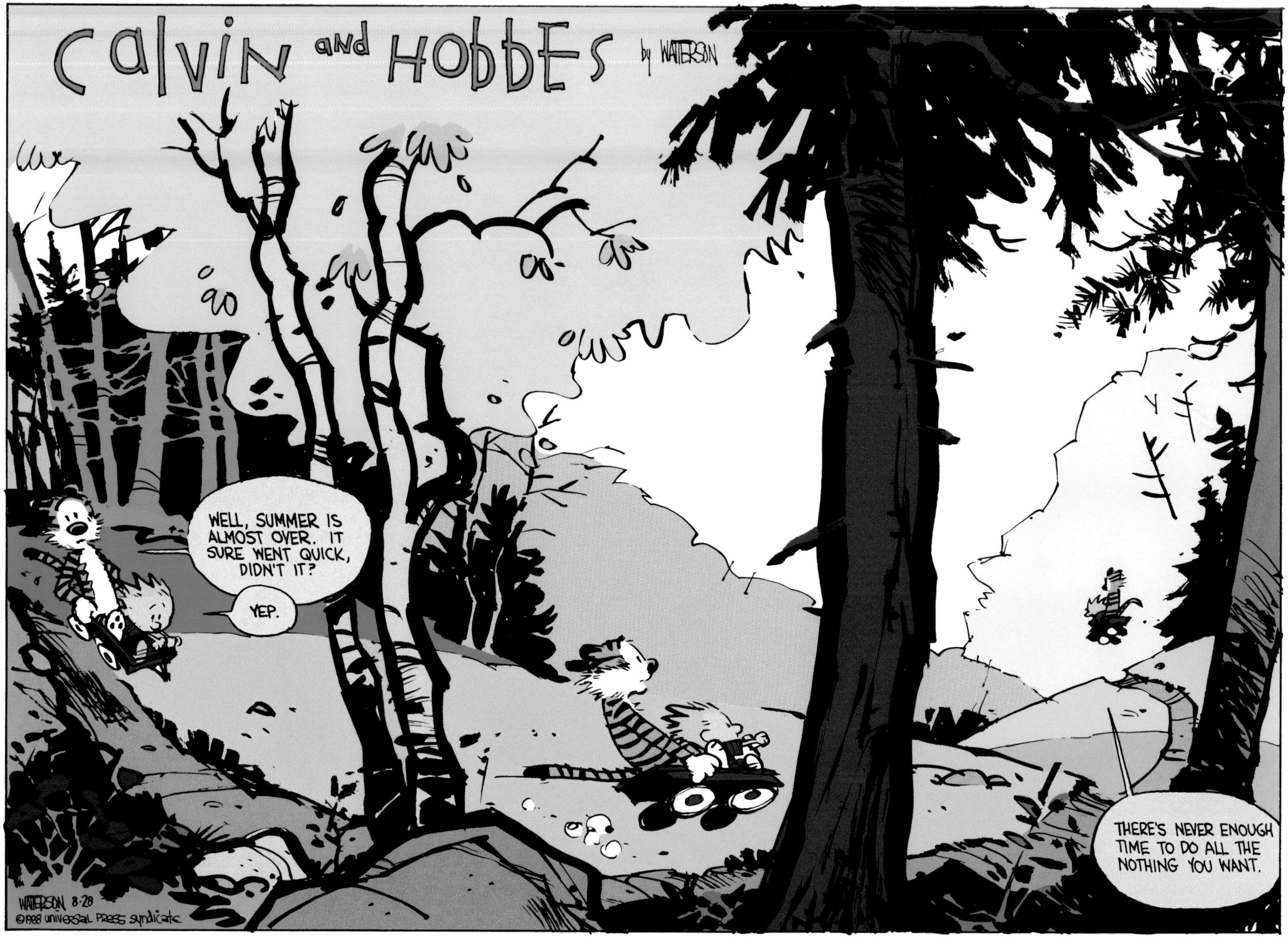
Calvin and HOBBES by WATTERSON
WELL, SUMMER IS ALMOST OVER. IT SURE WENT QUICK, DIDN'T IT?
YEP.
THERE'S NEVER ENOUGH TIME TO DO ALL THE NOTHING YOU WANT.
WATTERSON 8-28
©1988 Universal Press Syndicate

half page of the newspaper. Take off the top (the "throwaway panels") and the strip would run as a third of a page. Lop off another inch and a half, and the bottom part can be printed as a quarter page. The trick was to compose the drawing so that it would look intentional no matter how it was cropped.

This strip presented a further problem when it came time to be reprinted in a book collection. The strip, no matter how it's cropped, is horizontal, but the books had either a square or vertical format. The only solution was to redraw the whole thing in a vertical format for the books.

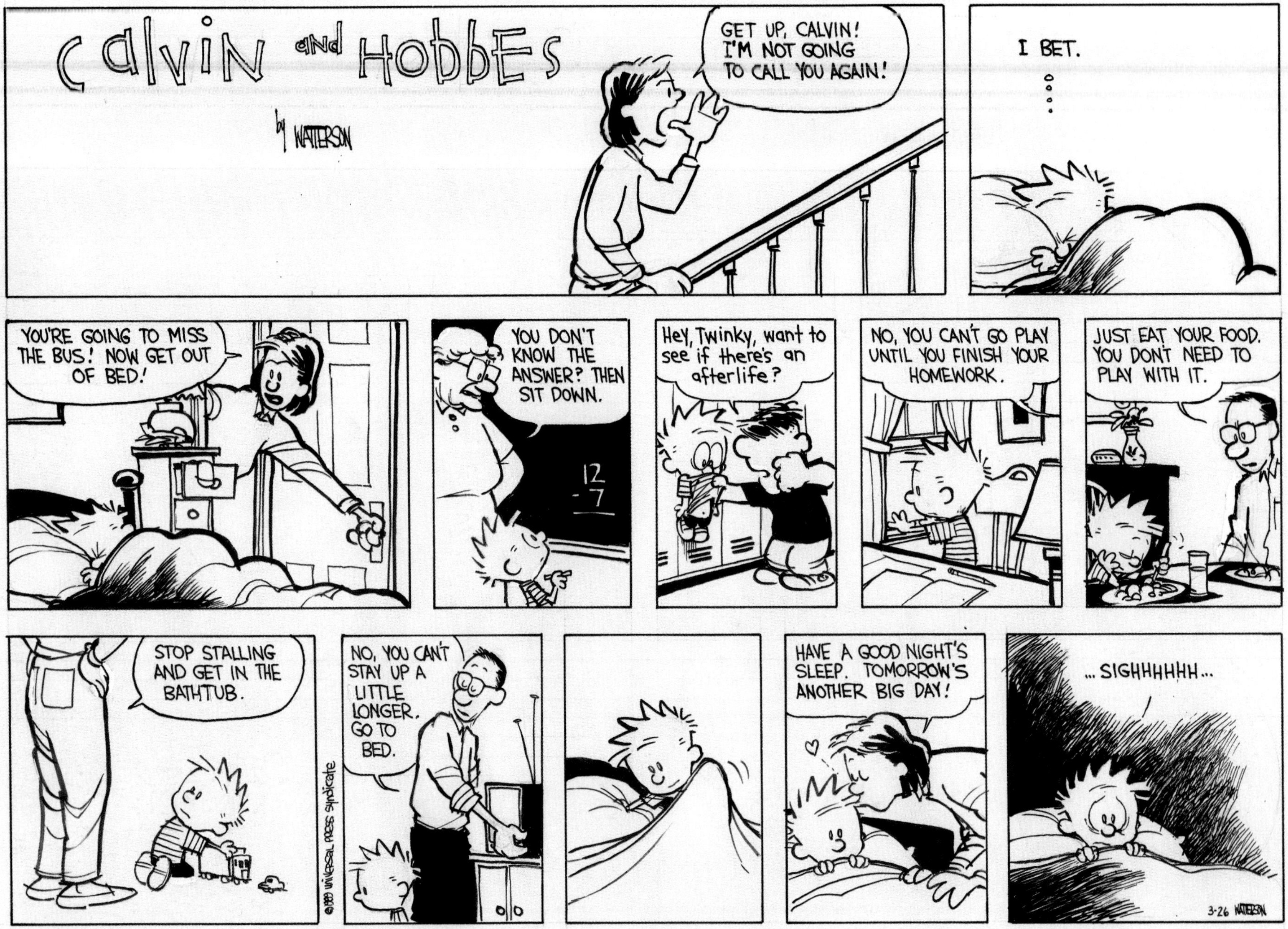
Calvin and Hobbes
by WATTERSON
GET UP, CALVIN! I'M NOT GOING TO CALL YOU AGAIN!
I BET.
YOU'RE GOING TO MISS THE BUS! NOW GET OUT OF BED!
YOU DON'T KNOW THE ANSWER? THEN SIT DOWN.
12
-7
Hey, Twinky, want to see if there's an afterlife?
NO, YOU CAN'T GO PLAY UNTIL YOU FINISH YOUR HOMEWORK.
JUST EAT YOUR FOOD. YOU DON'T NEED TO PLAY WITH IT.
STOP STALLING AND GET IN THE BATHTUB.
©1989 Universal Press Syndicate
NO, YOU CAN'T STAY UP A LITTLE LONGER. GO TO BED.
HAVE A GOOD NIGHT'S SLEEP. TOMORROW'S ANOTHER BIG DAY!
... SIGHHHHHH...
3-26 WATTERSON

MARCH 26, 1989

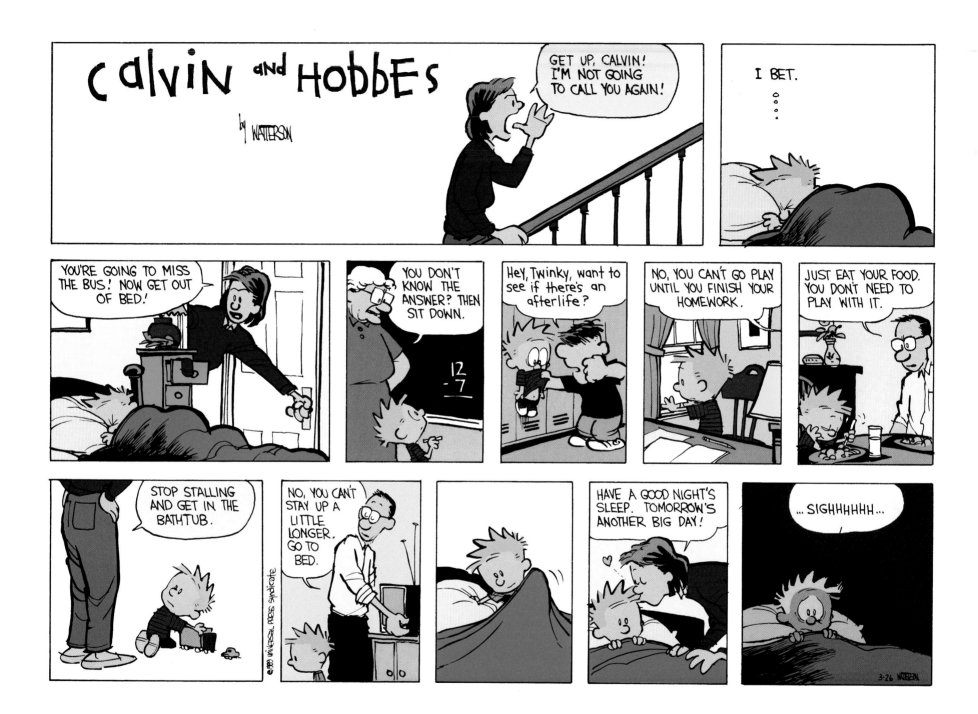

Several of my favorite Sunday strips depict an entire day. It's a slightly different way of telling the story, as there is no real plot. Instead, numerous isolated moments are illustrated, and the connection between them is largely made in hindsight. The Sunday strip offers enormous flexibility in storytelling, and this gradually attracted more and more of my interest.

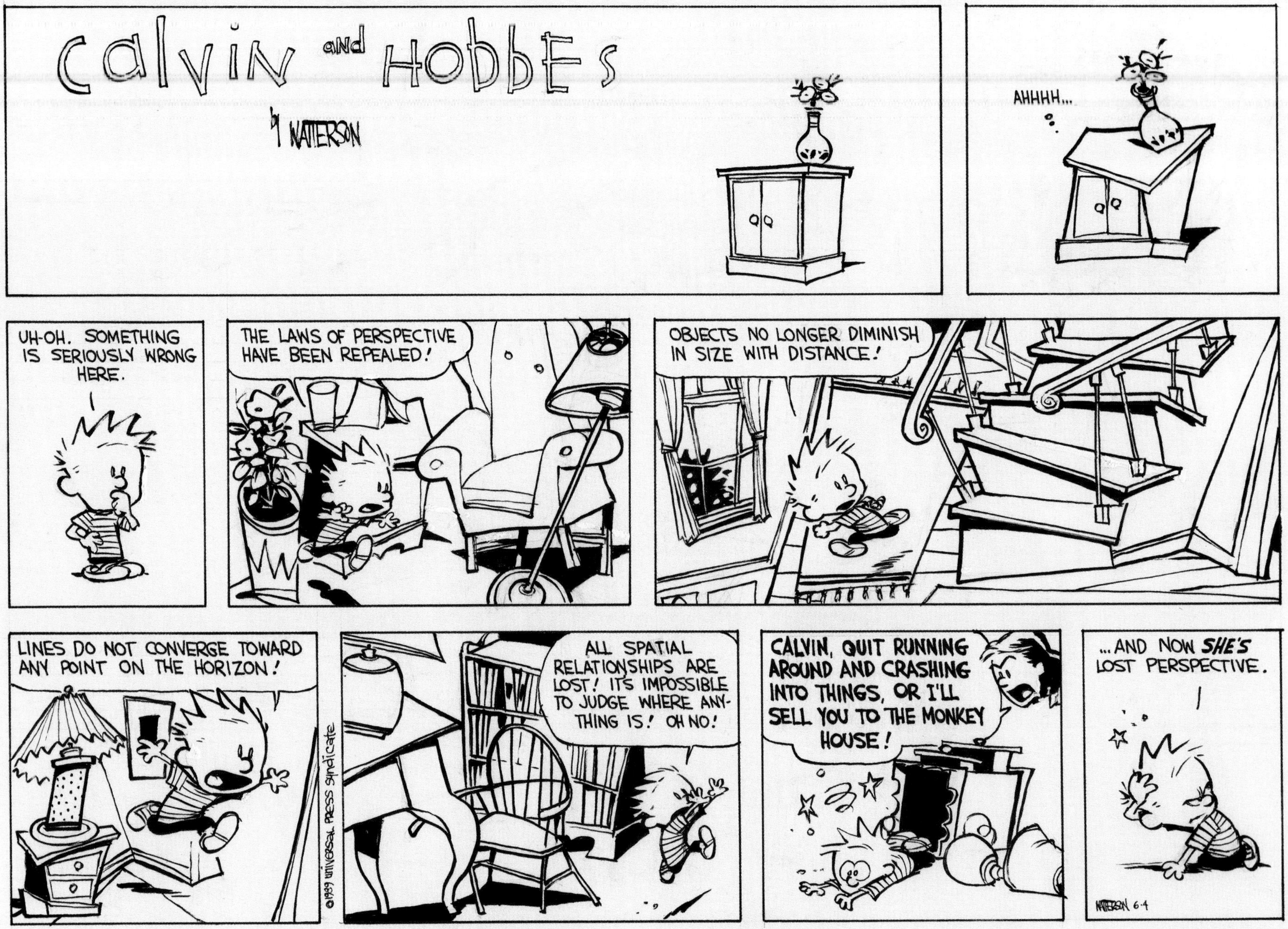
Calvin and HOBBES
by WATTERSON
AHHHH...
UH-OH. SOMETHING IS SERIOUSLY WRONG HERE.
THE LAWS OF PERSPECTIVE HAVE BEEN REPEALED!
OBJECTS NO LONGER DIMINISH IN SIZE WITH DISTANCE!
LINES DO NOT CONVERGE TOWARD ANY POINT ON THE HORIZON!
©1989 UNIVERSAL PRESS SYNDICATE
ALL SPATIAL RELATIONSHIPS ARE LOST! IT'S IMPOSSIBLE TO JUDGE WHERE ANYTHING IS! OH NO!
CALVIN, QUIT RUNNING AROUND AND CRASHING INTO THINGS, OR I'LL SELL YOU TO THE MONKEY HOUSE!
...AND NOW *SHE'S* LOST PERSPECTIVE.
WATTERSON 6-4

JUNE 4, 1989

It's surprisingly tricky to draw things exactly wrong, because you have to know the rules pretty well to break every single one. The strip was fun to draw.

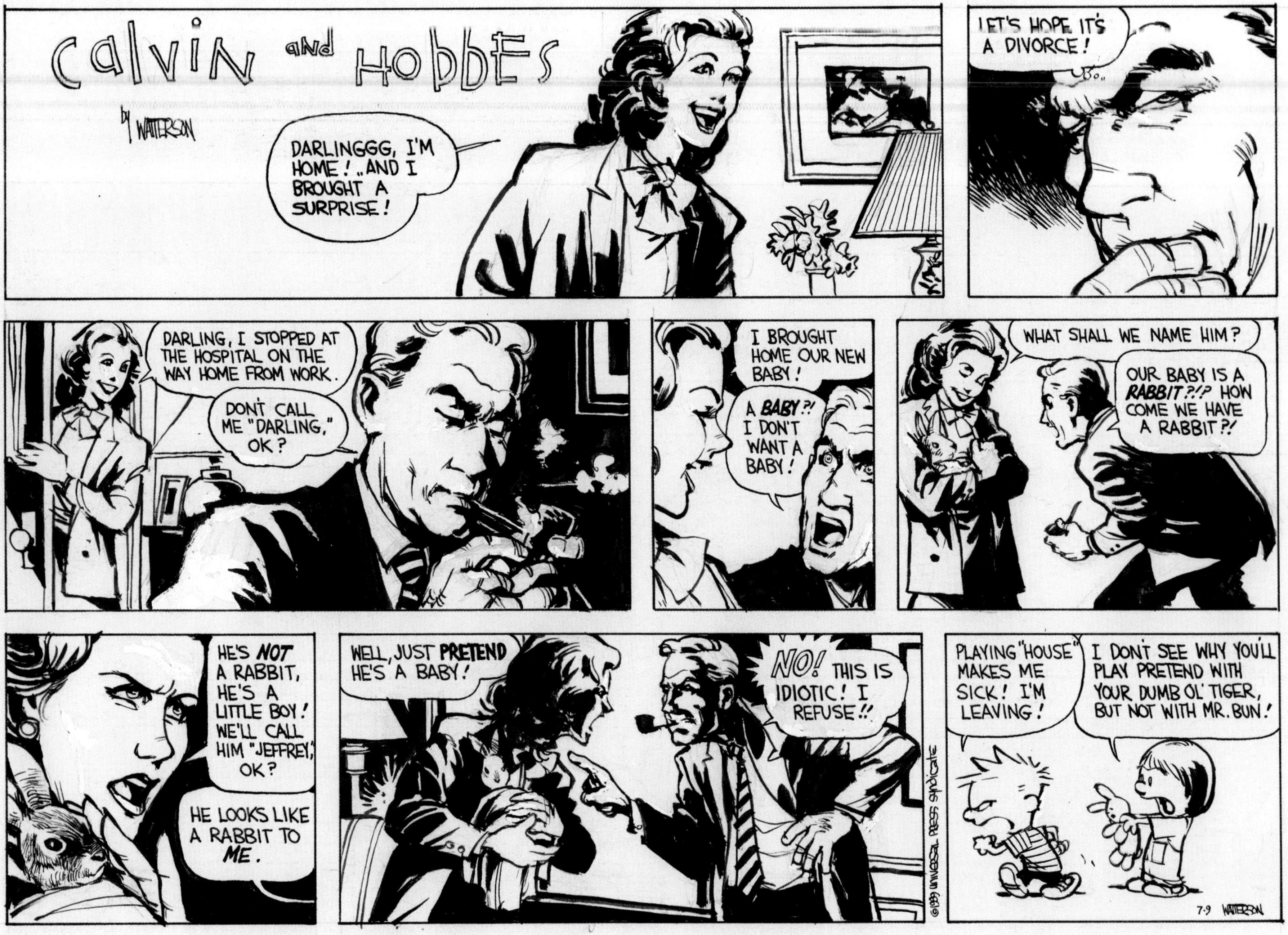
Calvin and HobbEs
by WATTERSON
DARLINGGG, I'M HOME! ..AND I BROUGHT A SURPRISE!
LET'S HOPE IT'S A DIVORCE!
DARLING, I STOPPED AT THE HOSPITAL ON THE WAY HOME FROM WORK.
DON'T CALL ME "DARLING," OK?
I BROUGHT HOME OUR NEW BABY!
A BABY?! I DON'T WANT A BABY!
WHAT SHALL WE NAME HIM?
OUR BABY IS A RABBIT?!? HOW COME WE HAVE A RABBIT?!
HE'S NOT A RABBIT, HE'S A LITTLE BOY! WE'LL CALL HIM "JEFFREY," OK?
HE LOOKS LIKE A RABBIT TO ME.
WELL, JUST PRETEND HE'S A BABY!
NO! THIS IS IDIOTIC! I REFUSE!!
©1989 UNIVERSAL PRESS SYNDICATE
PLAYING "HOUSE" MAKES ME SICK! I'M LEAVING!
I DON'T SEE WHY YOU'LL PLAY PRETEND WITH YOUR DUMB OL' TIGER, BUT NOT WITH MR. BUN!
7-9 WATTERSON

JULY 9, 1989

With every strip, my goal is to surprise myself. If I'm not surprised, the reader surely won't be either. The surprises are usually fairly small, so it's a real delight when an idea pops in from Pluto. The soap opera drawing style, the ludicrous dialogue, the bizarre storyline—every part of this strip confounded

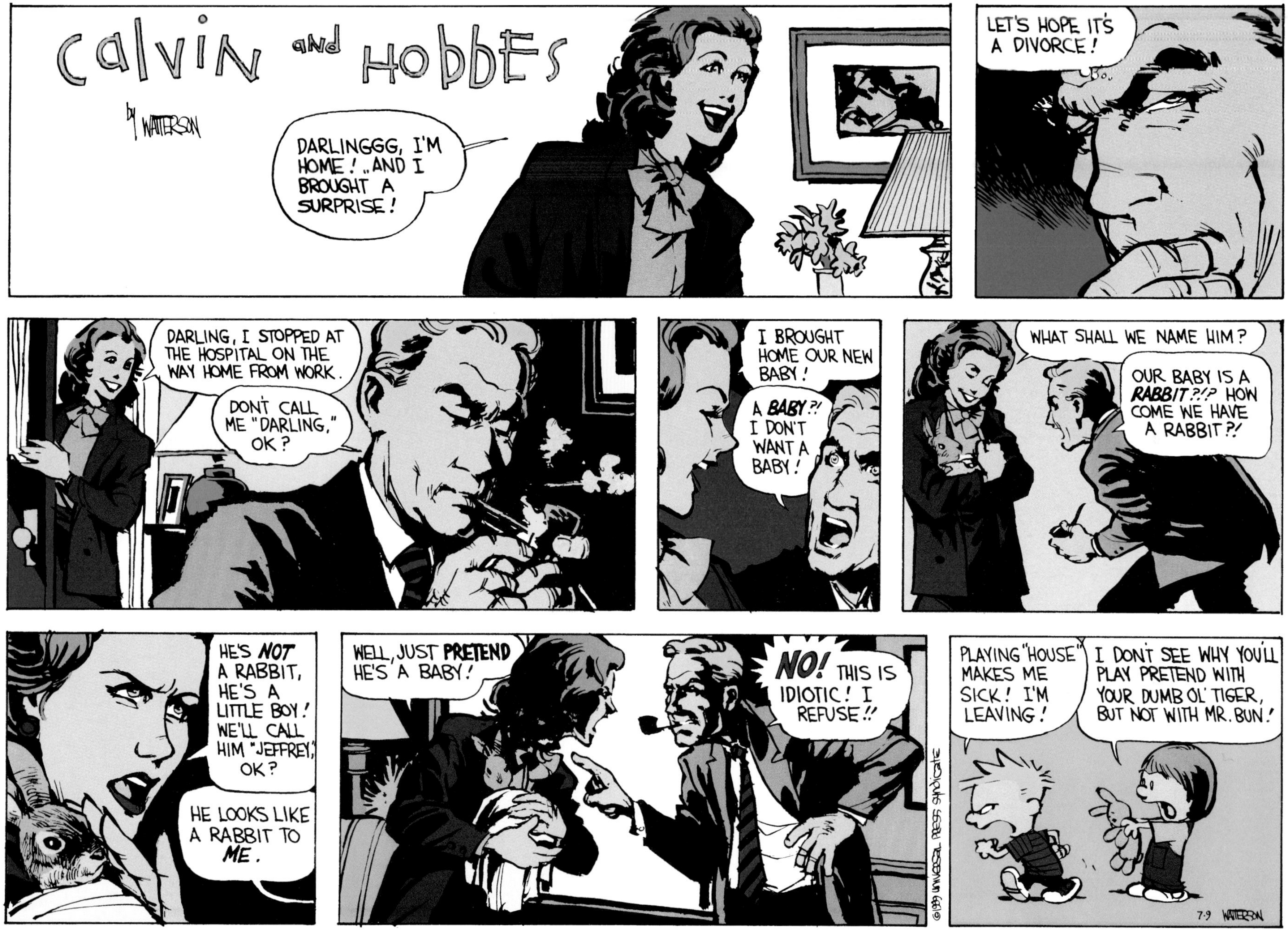
Calvin and Hobbes
by WATTERSON
DARLINGGG, I'M HOME! ..AND I BROUGHT A SURPRISE!
LET'S HOPE IT'S A DIVORCE!
DARLING, I STOPPED AT THE HOSPITAL ON THE WAY HOME FROM WORK.
DON'T CALL ME "DARLING," OK?
I BROUGHT HOME OUR NEW BABY!
A BABY?! I DON'T WANT A BABY!
WHAT SHALL WE NAME HIM?
OUR BABY IS A RABBIT?!? HOW COME WE HAVE A RABBIT?!
HE'S NOT A RABBIT, HE'S A LITTLE BOY! WE'LL CALL HIM "JEFFREY," OK?
HE LOOKS LIKE A RABBIT TO ME.
WELL, JUST PRETEND HE'S A BABY!
NO! THIS IS IDIOTIC! I REFUSE!!
PLAYING "HOUSE" MAKES ME SICK! I'M LEAVING!
I DON'T SEE WHY YOU'LL PLAY PRETEND WITH YOUR DUMB OL' TIGER, BUT NOT WITH MR. BUN!
©1989 UNIVERSAL PRESS SYNDICATE
7-9 WATTERSON

expectations. I hoped the reader would wonder for a second if *Calvin and Hobbes* had been replaced by another strip.

I wish I'd drawn this with a bit more flair in the line work. Some of the old continuity strips were very stylishly drawn and I'd like to have captured that. What I didn't know at that time was that many of those cartoonists drew very large. Doubling or tripling the size of my original would have helped.

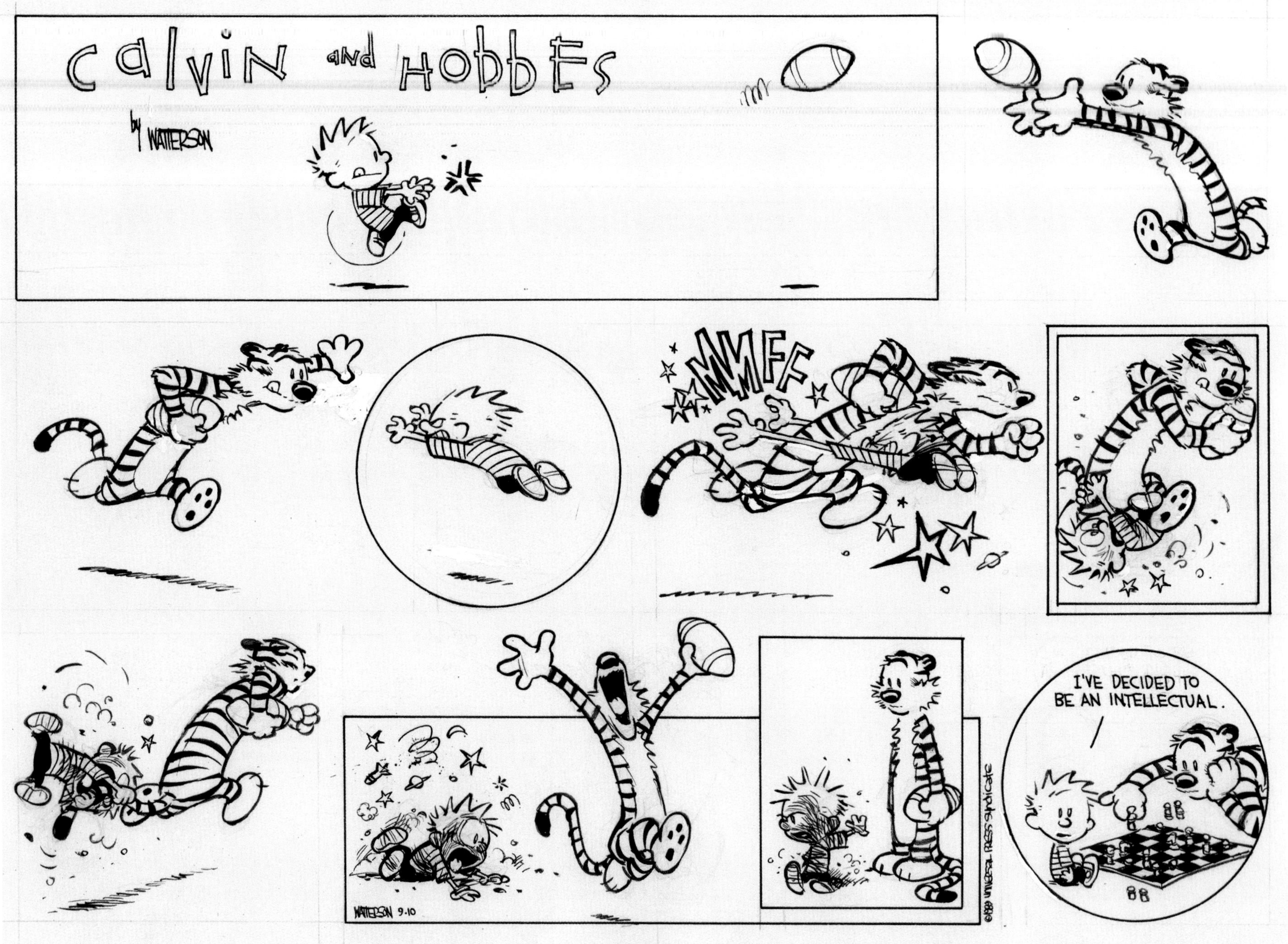
Calvin and HobbEs
by WATTERSON
MMMFF
WATTERSON 9.10
©1989 Universal Press Syndicate
I'VE DECIDED TO BE AN INTELLECTUAL.

September 10, 1989

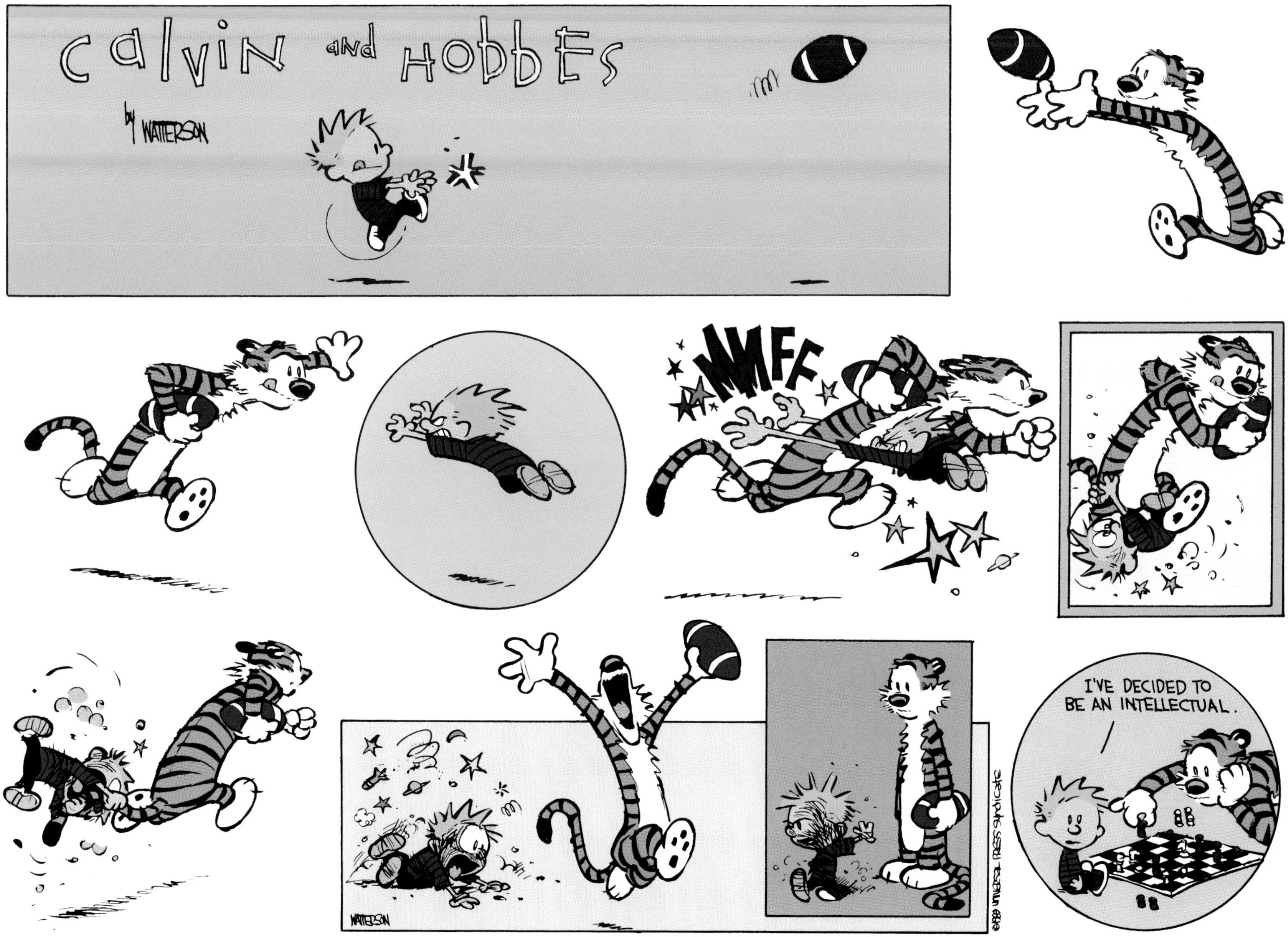
Calvin and Hobbes
by WATTERSON
WMFF
I'VE DECIDED TO BE AN INTELLECTUAL.
WATTERSON
©1989 Universal Press Syndicate

Here I was beginning to get a little more adventurous with panel layout, although I was still constrained by the mandated space divisions. The open spaces and different box shapes give the strip a looser feel. When the strip was restacked in some papers and in the book collections, the visual rhythm could go out of whack. Open panels might be next to each other, and boxed panels might all line up on the left side, and so on. The flexibility of the format always had a price.

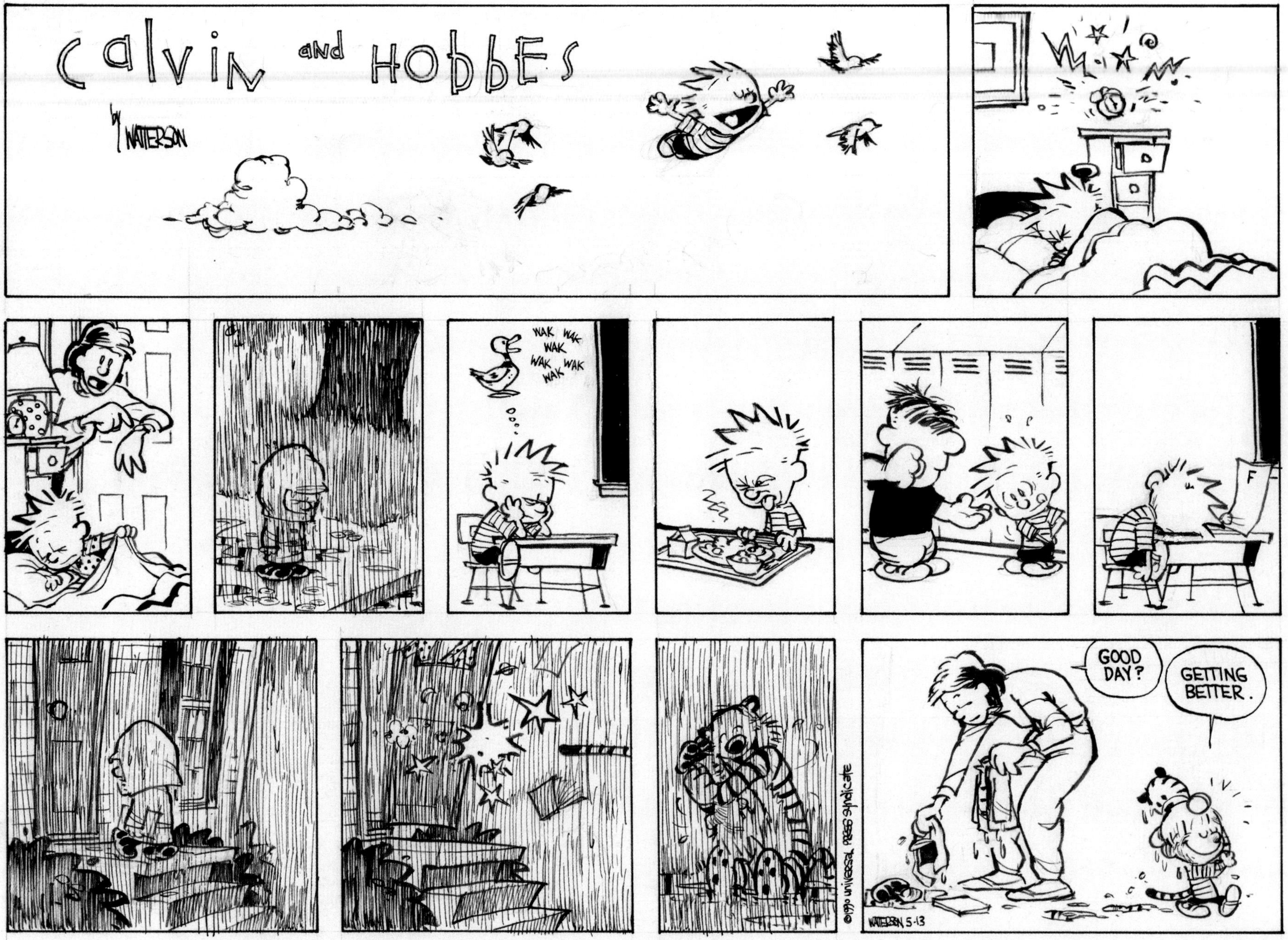
Calvin and Hobbes
by Watterson
WAK WAK WAK WAK WAK
F
GOOD DAY?
GETTING BETTER.
©1990 Universal Press Syndicate
WATTERSON 5-13

May 13, 1990

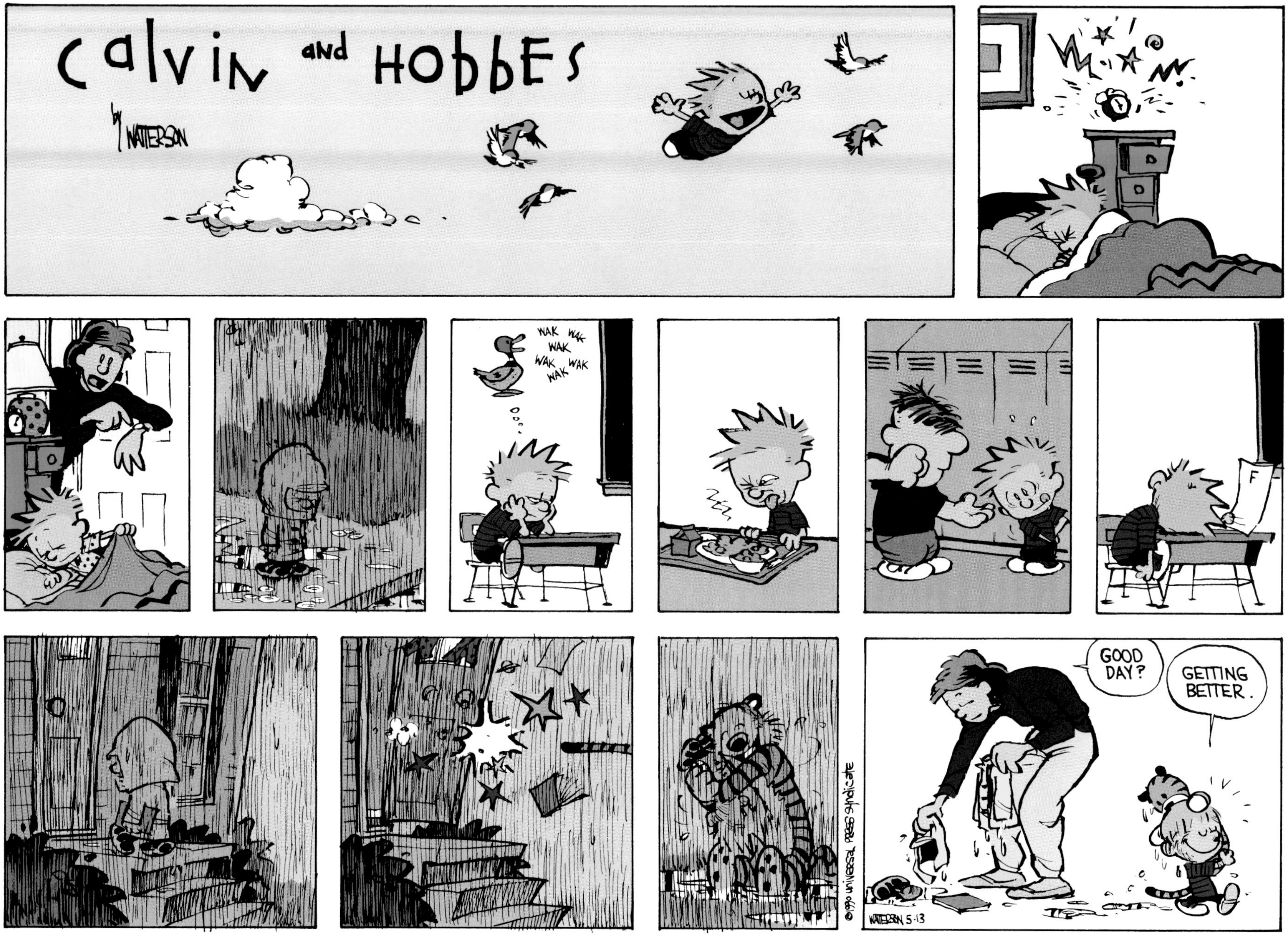
Calvin and HOBBES
by WATTERSON
WAK WAK
WAK
WAK WAK
WAK
F
©1990 Universal Press Syndicate
WATTERSON 5-13
GOOD DAY?
GETTING BETTER.

As I went along, I started eliminating dialogue from Sunday strips. Words are essential for certain kinds of ideas, but it is good to remember that cartoons are a visual medium, and pictures can do a great job of telling a story all by themselves.

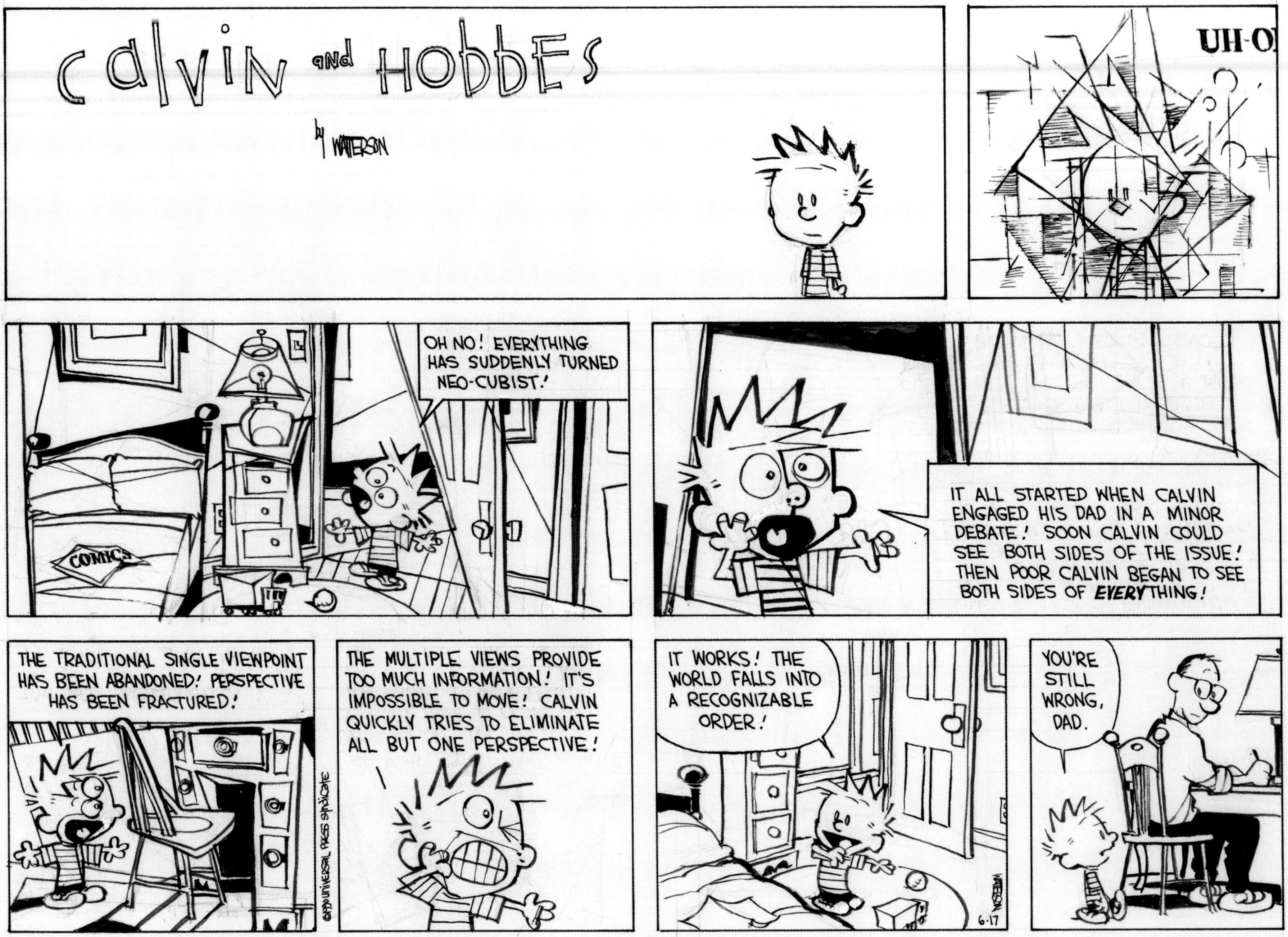
Calvin and HOBBES
by WATTERSON
UH-O
OH NO! EVERYTHING HAS SUDDENLY TURNED NEO-CUBIST!
COMICS
IT ALL STARTED WHEN CALVIN ENGAGED HIS DAD IN A MINOR DEBATE! SOON CALVIN COULD SEE BOTH SIDES OF THE ISSUE! THEN POOR CALVIN BEGAN TO SEE BOTH SIDES OF EVERYTHING!
THE TRADITIONAL SINGLE VIEWPOINT HAS BEEN ABANDONED! PERSPECTIVE HAS BEEN FRACTURED!
©1990 UNIVERSAL PRESS SYNDICATE
THE MULTIPLE VIEWS PROVIDE TOO MUCH INFORMATION! IT'S IMPOSSIBLE TO MOVE! CALVIN QUICKLY TRIES TO ELIMINATE ALL BUT ONE PERSPECTIVE!
IT WORKS! THE WORLD FALLS INTO A RECOGNIZABLE ORDER!
WATTERSON
6-17
YOU'RE STILL WRONG, DAD.

JUNE 17, 1990

Drawing this strip required a trip to the library to see some examples of cubist art, as I'd once again written material over my own head. The idea for this strip came from my tendency to examine issues until I'm incapacitated by the persuasiveness of all sides.

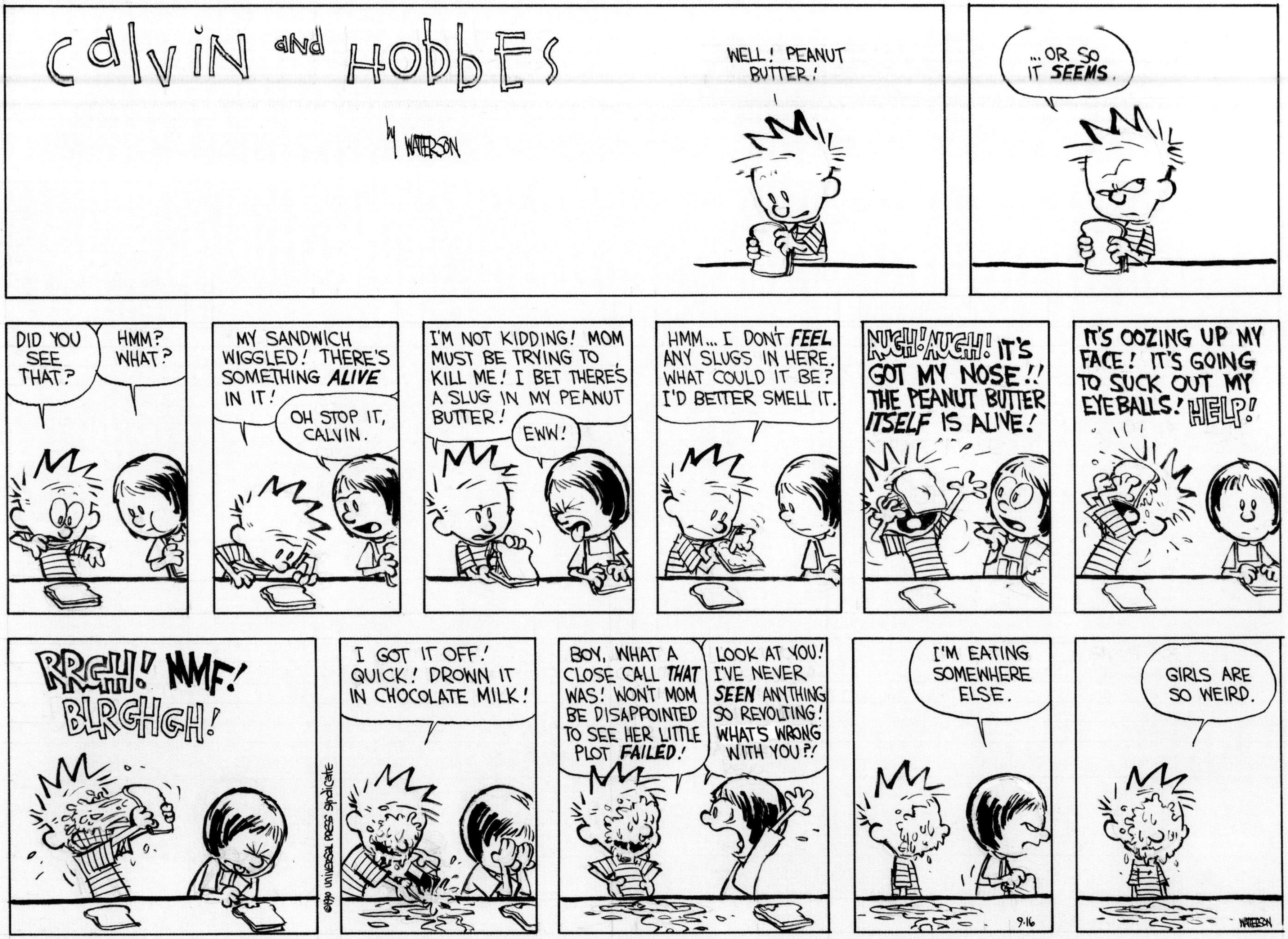
Calvin and Hobbes
by WATTERSON
WELL! PEANUT BUTTER!
...OR SO IT SEEMS.
DID YOU SEE THAT?
HMM? WHAT?
MY SANDWICH WIGGLED! THERE'S SOMETHING ALIVE IN IT!
OH STOP IT, CALVIN.
I'M NOT KIDDING! MOM MUST BE TRYING TO KILL ME! I BET THERE'S A SLUG IN MY PEANUT BUTTER!
EWW!
HMM... I DON'T FEEL ANY SLUGS IN HERE. WHAT COULD IT BE? I'D BETTER SMELL IT.
AUGH! AUGH! IT'S GOT MY NOSE!! THE PEANUT BUTTER ITSELF IS ALIVE!
IT'S OOZING UP MY FACE! IT'S GOING TO SUCK OUT MY EYEBALLS! HELP!
RRGH! MMF! BLRGHGH!
©1990 UNIVERSAL PRESS SYNDICATE
I GOT IT OFF! QUICK! DROWN IT IN CHOCOLATE MILK!
BOY, WHAT A CLOSE CALL THAT WAS! WON'T MOM BE DISAPPOINTED TO SEE HER LITTLE PLOT FAILED!
LOOK AT YOU! I'VE NEVER SEEN ANYTHING SO REVOLTING! WHAT'S WRONG WITH YOU?!
I'M EATING SOMEWHERE ELSE.
9·16
GIRLS ARE SO WEIRD.
WATTERSON

SEPTEMBER 16, 1990

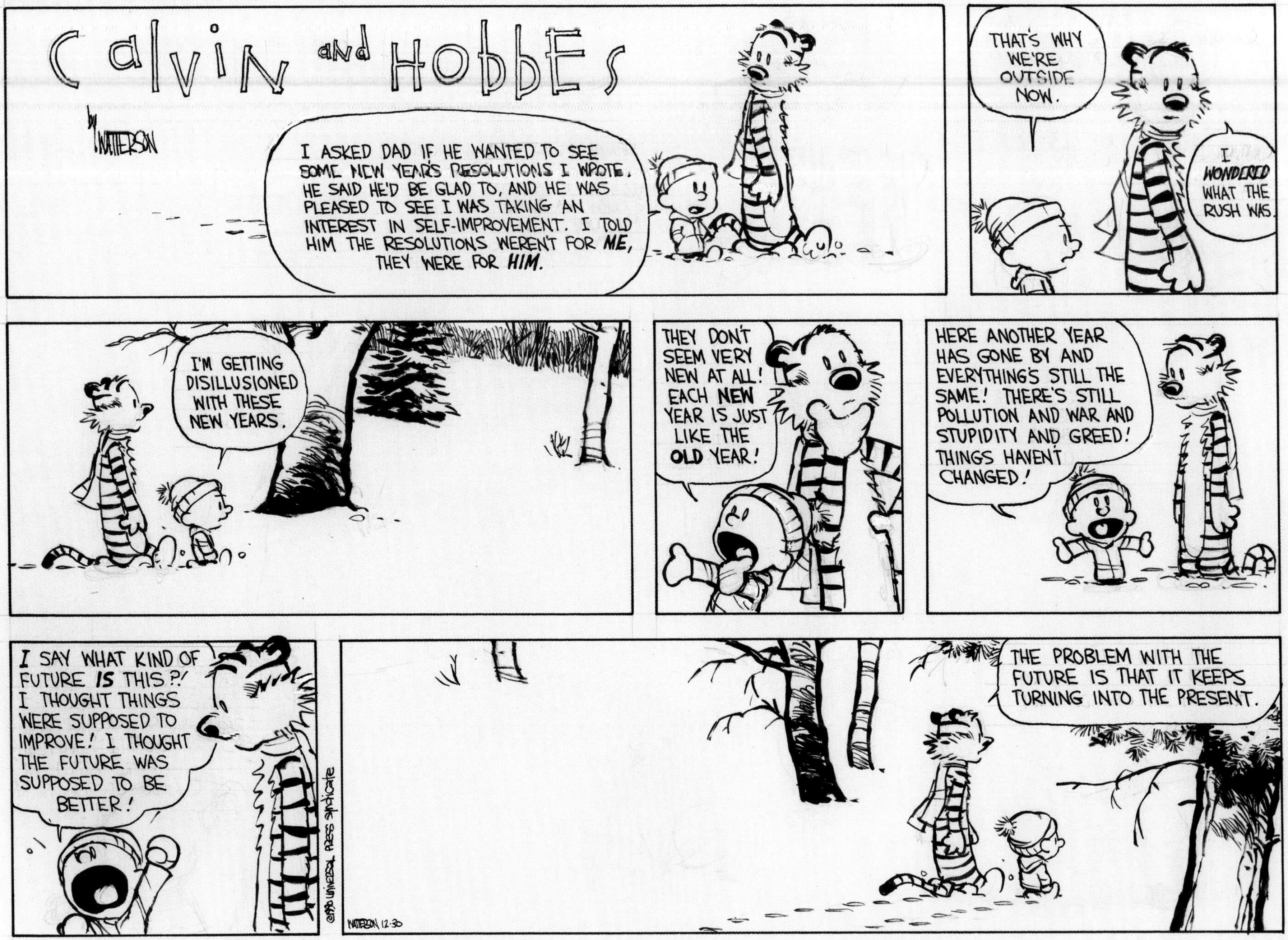
Calvin and Hobbes
by Watterson
I ASKED DAD IF HE WANTED TO SEE SOME NEW YEAR'S RESOLUTIONS I WROTE. HE SAID HE'D BE GLAD TO, AND HE WAS PLEASED TO SEE I WAS TAKING AN INTEREST IN SELF-IMPROVEMENT. I TOLD HIM THE RESOLUTIONS WEREN'T FOR ME, THEY WERE FOR HIM.
THAT'S WHY WE'RE OUTSIDE NOW.
I WONDERED WHAT THE RUSH WAS.
I'M GETTING DISILLUSIONED WITH THESE NEW YEARS.
THEY DON'T SEEM VERY NEW AT ALL! EACH NEW YEAR IS JUST LIKE THE OLD YEAR!
HERE ANOTHER YEAR HAS GONE BY AND EVERYTHING'S STILL THE SAME! THERE'S STILL POLLUTION AND WAR AND STUPIDITY AND GREED! THINGS HAVEN'T CHANGED!
I SAY WHAT KIND OF FUTURE IS THIS?! I THOUGHT THINGS WERE SUPPOSED TO IMPROVE! I THOUGHT THE FUTURE WAS SUPPOSED TO BE BETTER!
©1990 Universal Press Syndicate
WATTERSON 12-30
THE PROBLEM WITH THE FUTURE IS THAT IT KEEPS TURNING INTO THE PRESENT.

DECEMBER 30, 1990

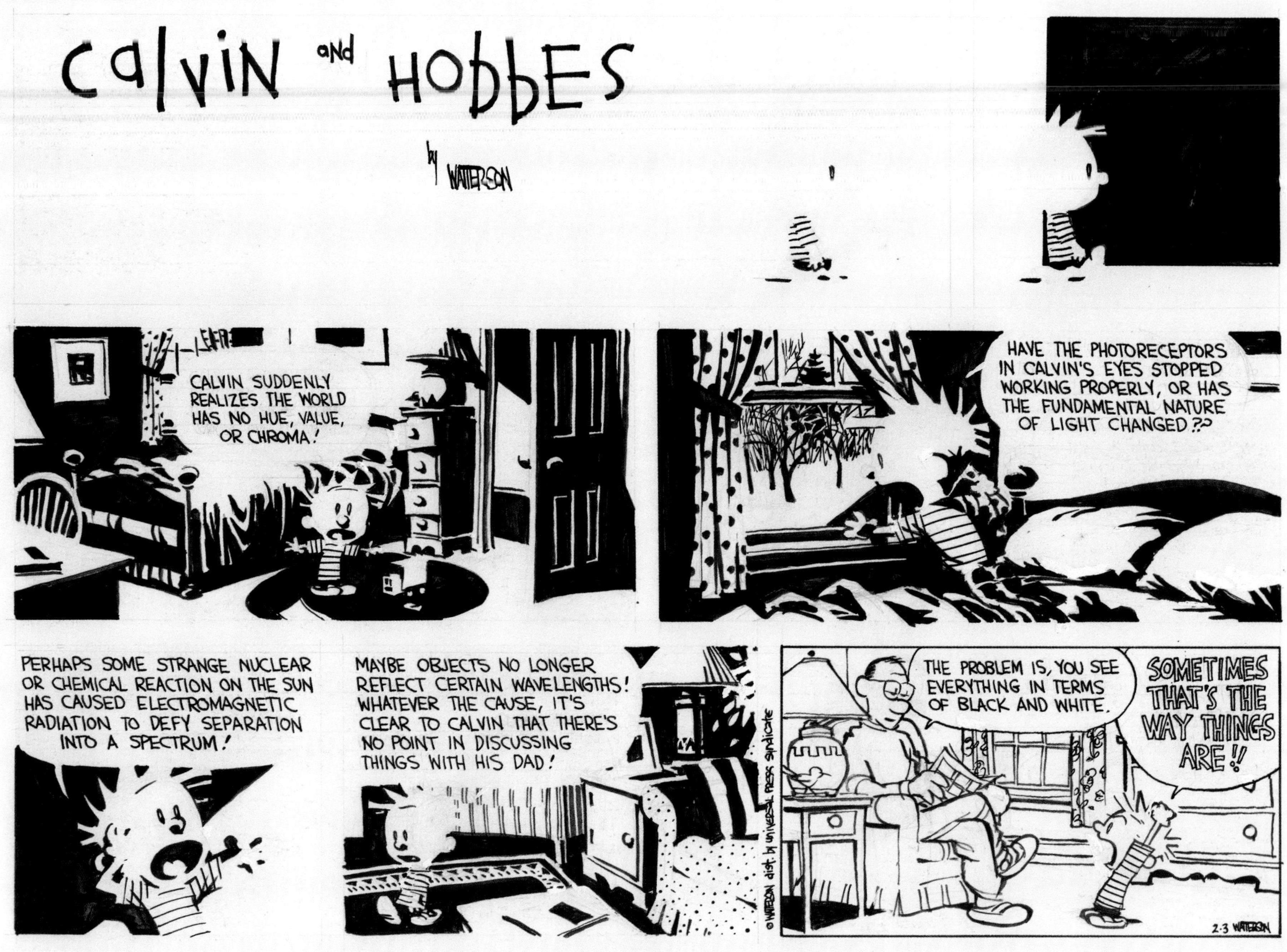

Calvin and Hobbes
by WATTERSON
CALVIN SUDDENLY REALIZES THE WORLD HAS NO HUE, VALUE, OR CHROMA!
HAVE THE PHOTORECEPTORS IN CALVIN'S EYES STOPPED WORKING PROPERLY, OR HAS THE FUNDAMENTAL NATURE OF LIGHT CHANGED?!
PERHAPS SOME STRANGE NUCLEAR OR CHEMICAL REACTION ON THE SUN HAS CAUSED ELECTROMAGNETIC RADIATION TO DEFY SEPARATION INTO A SPECTRUM!
MAYBE OBJECTS NO LONGER REFLECT CERTAIN WAVELENGTHS! WHATEVER THE CAUSE, IT'S CLEAR TO CALVIN THAT THERE'S NO POINT IN DISCUSSING THINGS WITH HIS DAD!
© WATTERSON dist. by universal press syndicate
THE PROBLEM IS, YOU SEE EVERYTHING IN TERMS OF BLACK AND WHITE.
SOMETIMES THAT'S THE WAY THINGS ARE!!
2·3 WATTERSON

FEBRUARY 3, 1991

Unlike most art, comics often lose something in the original. In newspapers the last panel was in color.

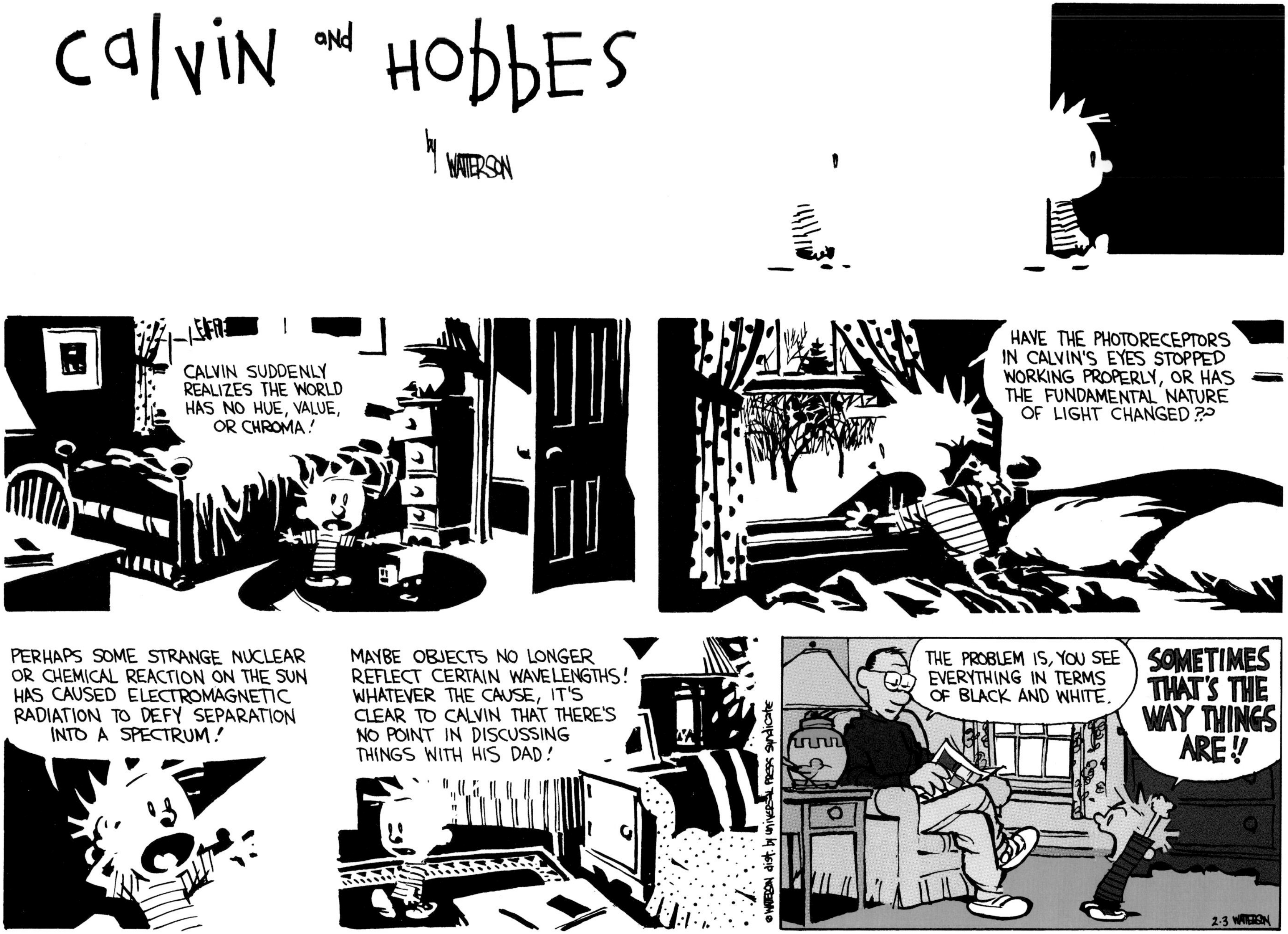
Calvin and Hobbes
by WATTERSON
CALVIN SUDDENLY REALIZES THE WORLD HAS NO HUE, VALUE, OR CHROMA!
HAVE THE PHOTORECEPTORS IN CALVIN'S EYES STOPPED WORKING PROPERLY, OR HAS THE FUNDAMENTAL NATURE OF LIGHT CHANGED?
PERHAPS SOME STRANGE NUCLEAR OR CHEMICAL REACTION ON THE SUN HAS CAUSED ELECTROMAGNETIC RADIATION TO DEFY SEPARATION INTO A SPECTRUM!
MAYBE OBJECTS NO LONGER REFLECT CERTAIN WAVELENGTHS! WHATEVER THE CAUSE, IT'S CLEAR TO CALVIN THAT THERE'S NO POINT IN DISCUSSING THINGS WITH HIS DAD!
THE PROBLEM IS, YOU SEE EVERYTHING IN TERMS OF BLACK AND WHITE.
SOMETIMES THAT'S THE WAY THINGS ARE!!
© WATTERSON dist. by Universal Press Syndicate
2-3 WATTERSON

To draw this strip, I not only avoided color and halftones, I avoided outlines. As the top "throwaway" panels illustrate, the placement of black is crucial to making the pictures comprehensible.
During my fight to prevent *Calvin and Hobbes* from being turned into licensed merchandise, I was accused of having a black-and-white view of the issue. The arguing dragged on for years and was very frustrating and unpleasant, so it was a bit of a release to get an interesting strip idea out of the conflict.

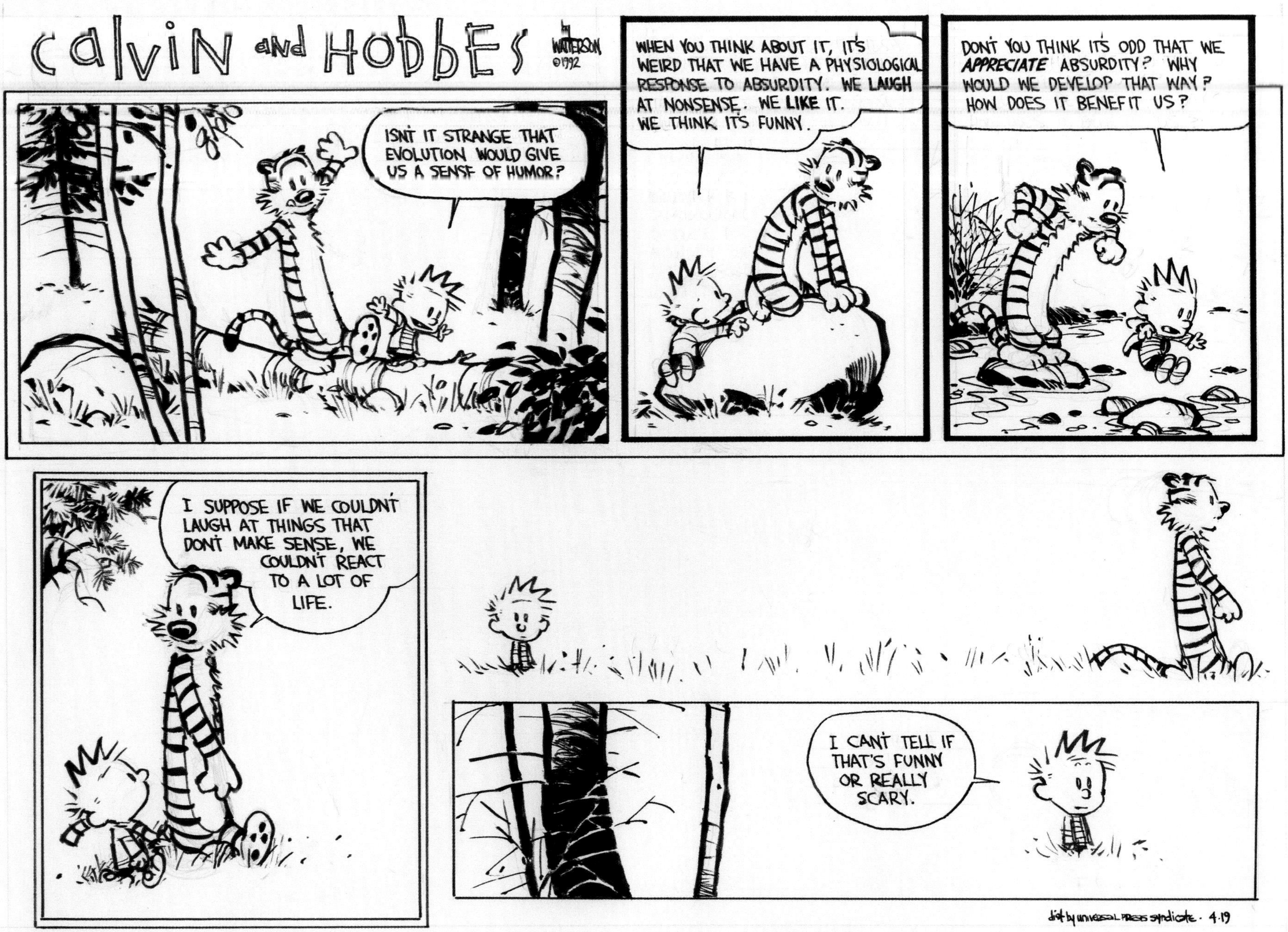
Calvin and Hobbes
by WATTERSON ©1992
ISN'T IT STRANGE THAT EVOLUTION WOULD GIVE US A SENSE OF HUMOR?
WHEN YOU THINK ABOUT IT, IT'S WEIRD THAT WE HAVE A PHYSIOLOGICAL RESPONSE TO ABSURDITY. WE LAUGH AT NONSENSE. WE LIKE IT. WE THINK IT'S FUNNY.
DON'T YOU THINK IT'S ODD THAT WE APPRECIATE ABSURDITY? WHY WOULD WE DEVELOP THAT WAY? HOW DOES IT BENEFIT US?
I SUPPOSE IF WE COULDN'T LAUGH AT THINGS THAT DON'T MAKE SENSE, WE COULDN'T REACT TO A LOT OF LIFE.
I CAN'T TELL IF THAT'S FUNNY OR REALLY SCARY.
dist by universal press syndicate · 4·19

APRIL 19, 1992

This strip was done in the new half–page format. It has only six panels, but I think the space is used attractively.

To an editor, space may be money, but to a cartoonist, space is time. Space provides the tempo and rhythm of the strip. Used well, it directs the eye to speed up or linger. The long drawing of Hobbes walking away is a sort of visual brake. It's empty, so the eye rests there and the panel creates a pause.

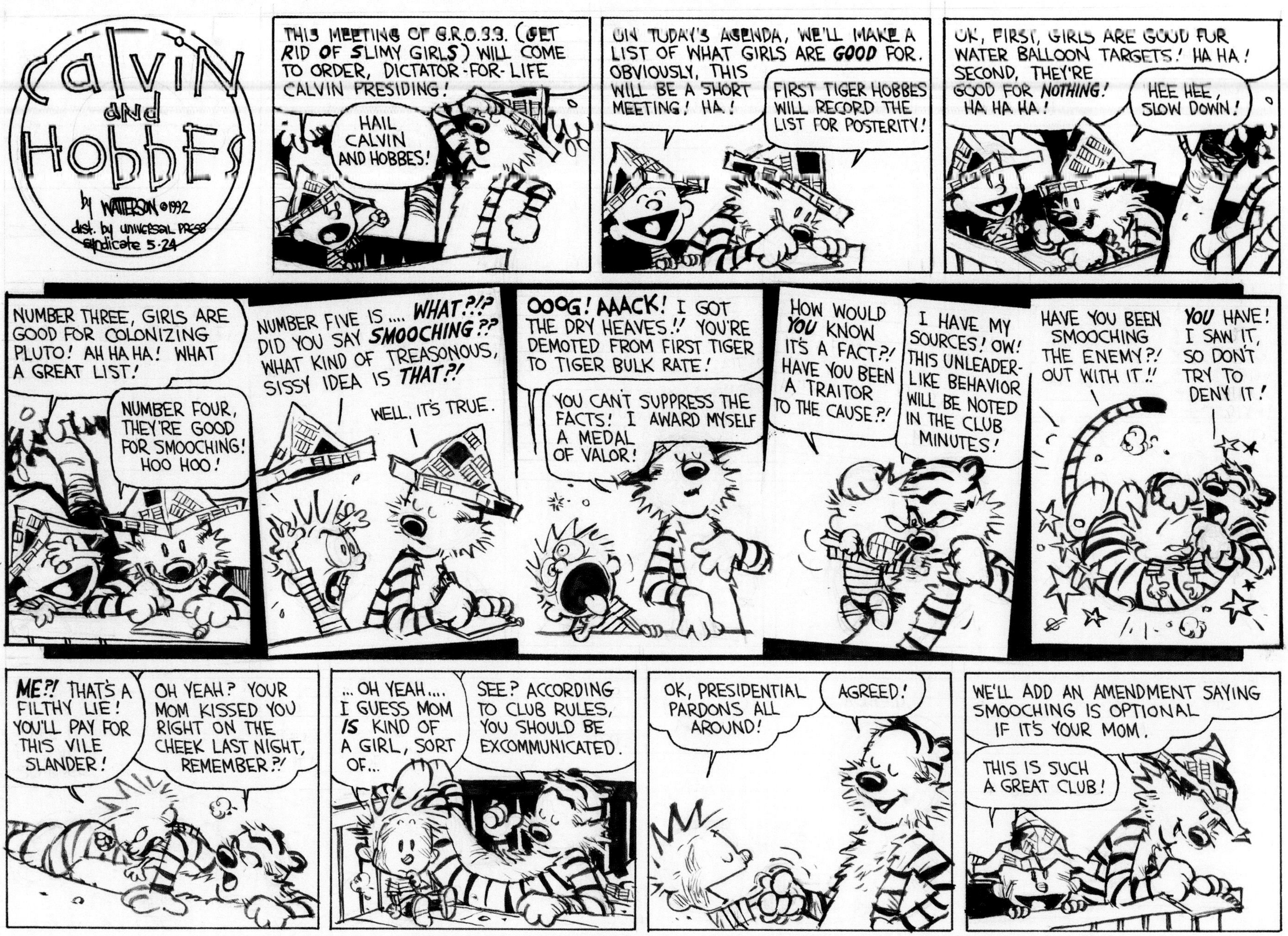

Calvin and Hobbes
by WATTERSON ©1992
dist. by UNIVERSAL PRESS syndicate 5-24
THIS MEETING OF G.R.O.S.S. (GET RID OF SLIMY GIRLS) WILL COME TO ORDER, DICTATOR-FOR-LIFE CALVIN PRESIDING!
HAIL CALVIN AND HOBBES!
ON TODAY'S AGENDA, WE'LL MAKE A LIST OF WHAT GIRLS ARE GOOD FOR. OBVIOUSLY, THIS WILL BE A SHORT MEETING! HA!
FIRST TIGER HOBBES WILL RECORD THE LIST FOR POSTERITY!
OK, FIRST, GIRLS ARE GOOD FOR WATER BALLOON TARGETS! HA HA! SECOND, THEY'RE GOOD FOR NOTHING! HA HA HA!
HEE HEE, SLOW DOWN!
NUMBER THREE, GIRLS ARE GOOD FOR COLONIZING PLUTO! AH HA HA! WHAT A GREAT LIST!
NUMBER FOUR, THEY'RE GOOD FOR SMOOCHING! HOO HOO!
NUMBER FIVE IS .... WHAT?!? DID YOU SAY SMOOCHING?? WHAT KIND OF TREASONOUS, SISSY IDEA IS THAT?!
WELL, IT'S TRUE.
OOOG! AAACK! I GOT THE DRY HEAVES!! YOU'RE DEMOTED FROM FIRST TIGER TO TIGER BULK RATE!
YOU CAN'T SUPPRESS THE FACTS! I AWARD MYSELF A MEDAL OF VALOR!
HOW WOULD YOU KNOW IT'S A FACT?! HAVE YOU BEEN A TRAITOR TO THE CAUSE?!
I HAVE MY SOURCES! OW! THIS UNLEADER-LIKE BEHAVIOR WILL BE NOTED IN THE CLUB MINUTES!
HAVE YOU BEEN SMOOCHING THE ENEMY?! OUT WITH IT!!
YOU HAVE! I SAW IT, SO DON'T TRY TO DENY IT!
ME?! THAT'S A FILTHY LIE! YOU'LL PAY FOR THIS VILE SLANDER!
OH YEAH? YOUR MOM KISSED YOU RIGHT ON THE CHEEK LAST NIGHT, REMEMBER?!
... OH YEAH.... I GUESS MOM IS KIND OF A GIRL, SORT OF...
SEE? ACCORDING TO CLUB RULES, YOU SHOULD BE EXCOMMUNICATED.
OK, PRESIDENTIAL PARDONS ALL AROUND!
AGREED!
WE'LL ADD AN AMENDMENT SAYING SMOOCHING IS OPTIONAL IF IT'S YOUR MOM.
THIS IS SUCH A GREAT CLUB!

MAY 24, 1992

Although conservative in panel layout, I could now use the entire space without threat of having panels removed or rearranged for different newspaper formats. Readers would finally see everything I drew, exactly the way I drew it.

There are lots of words in this strip. That's always somewhat visually oppressive, but the dialogue has some spirit and I think there's enough going on to reward the reader's patience. The color helped enliven the drawings too. I'd have used more black if this were intended to remain uncolored.

I usually saved the G.R.O.S.S. strips for longer stories in the dailies, but the new space in the Sundays was an irresistible opportunity to let the characters bounce off each other for a while.

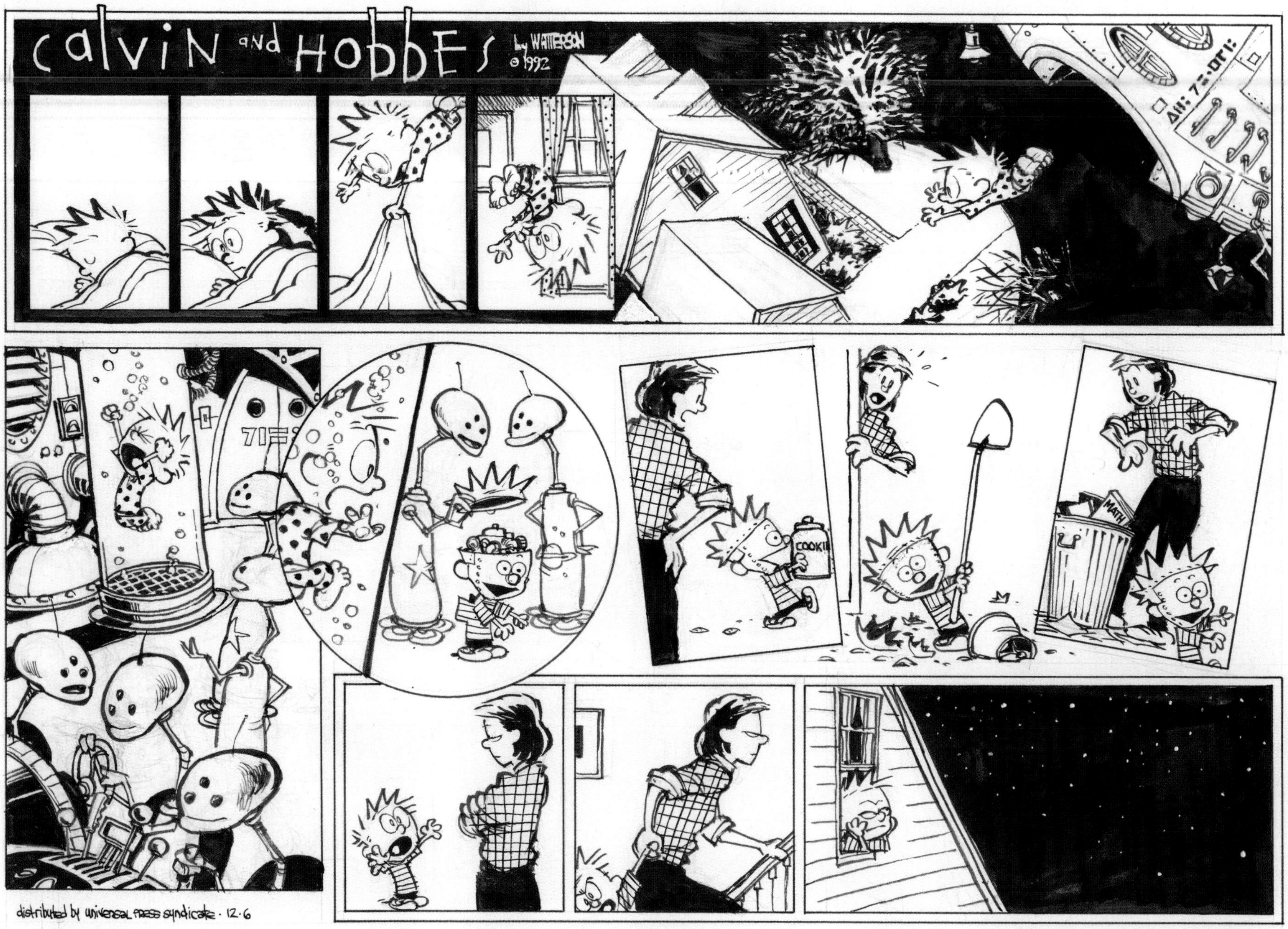
Calvin and HOBBES
by WATTERSON
© 1992
COOKIE
MATH
distributed by universal press syndicate · 12·6

DECEMBER 6, 1992

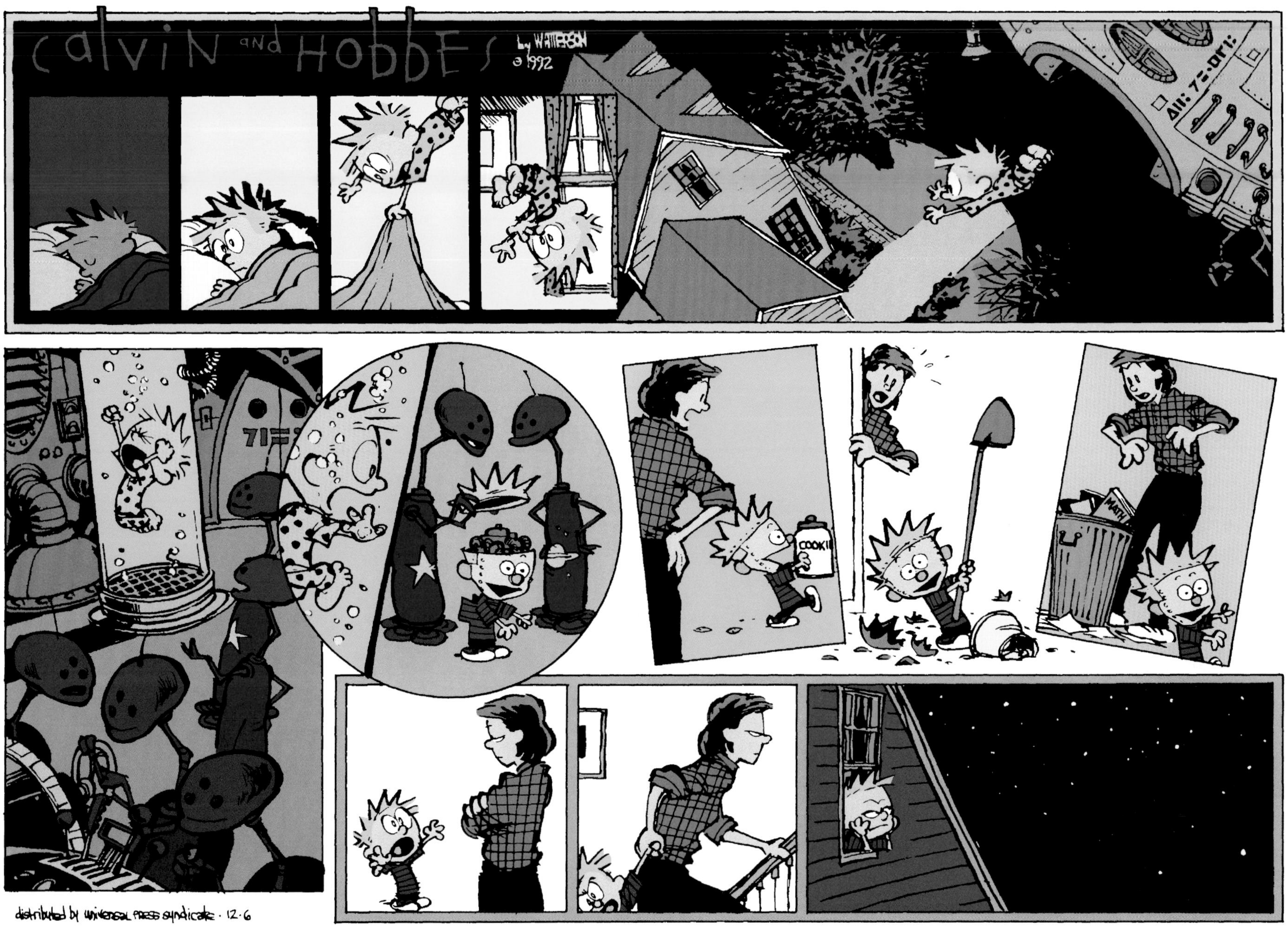
calvin and HOBBES
by WATTERSON
© 1992
COOKI
MATH
distributed by universal press syndicate · 12·6

I think much of the fun in this strip comes from the details in the drawing. The visual richness encourages you to look at the strip for a moment even after you get the joke. This pleasure is largely lost now that newspapers print the comics so small.

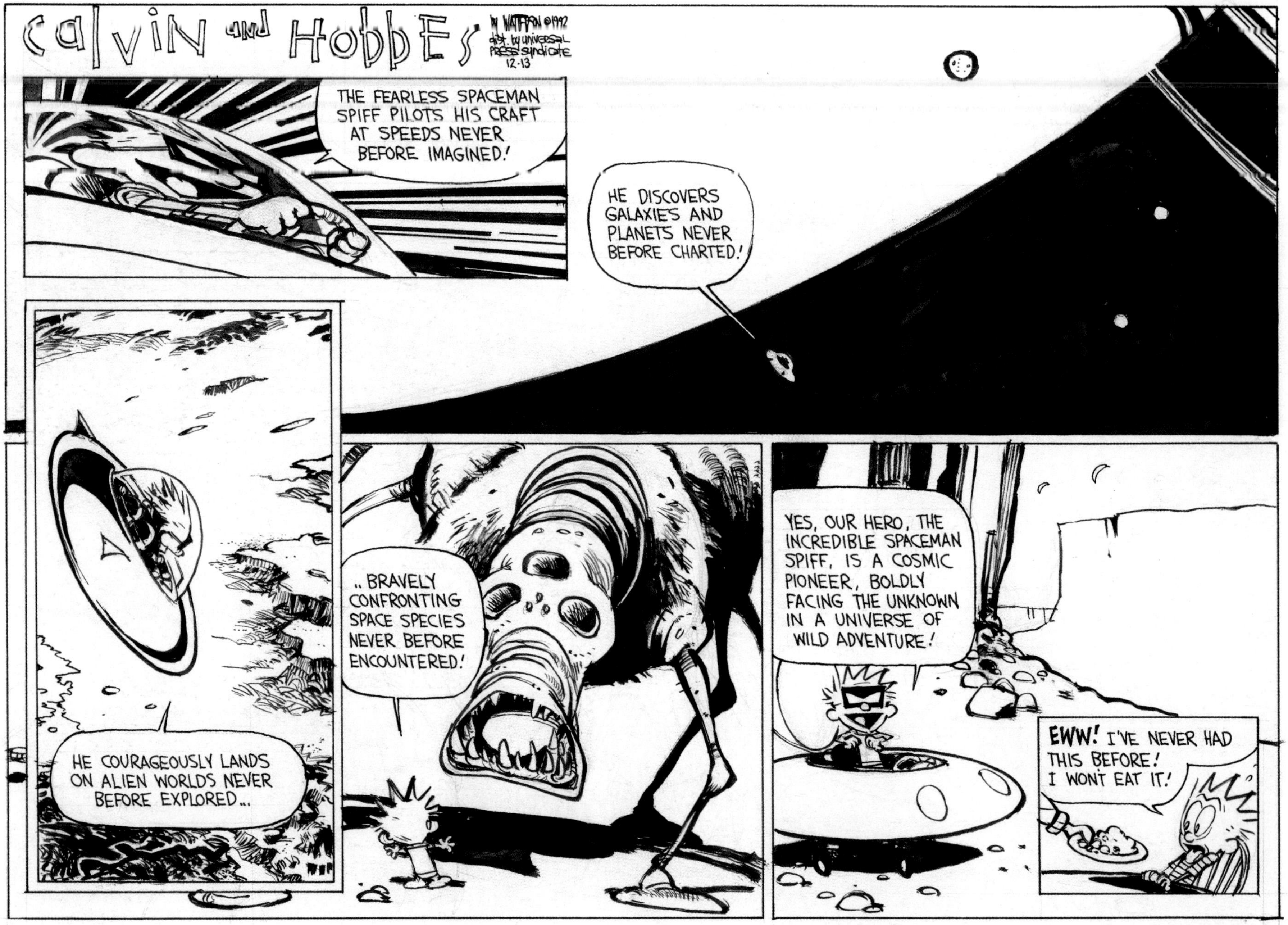
Calvin and Hobbes
by WATTERSON ©1992 dist. by universal press syndicate 12-13
THE FEARLESS SPACEMAN SPIFF PILOTS HIS CRAFT AT SPEEDS NEVER BEFORE IMAGINED!
HE DISCOVERS GALAXIES AND PLANETS NEVER BEFORE CHARTED!
HE COURAGEOUSLY LANDS ON ALIEN WORLDS NEVER BEFORE EXPLORED...
.. BRAVELY CONFRONTING SPACE SPECIES NEVER BEFORE ENCOUNTERED!
YES, OUR HERO, THE INCREDIBLE SPACEMAN SPIFF, IS A COSMIC PIONEER, BOLDLY FACING THE UNKNOWN IN A UNIVERSE OF WILD ADVENTURE!
EWW! I'VE NEVER HAD THIS BEFORE! I WON'T EAT IT!

December 13, 1992

With the large Sundays, I felt that *Calvin and Hobbes* kicked into high gear. The large format not only encouraged new ways of presenting ideas, it forced me to push the drawings, to make Calvin's world as bold and energetic as I could. I felt the strip finally looked the way it did in my head.

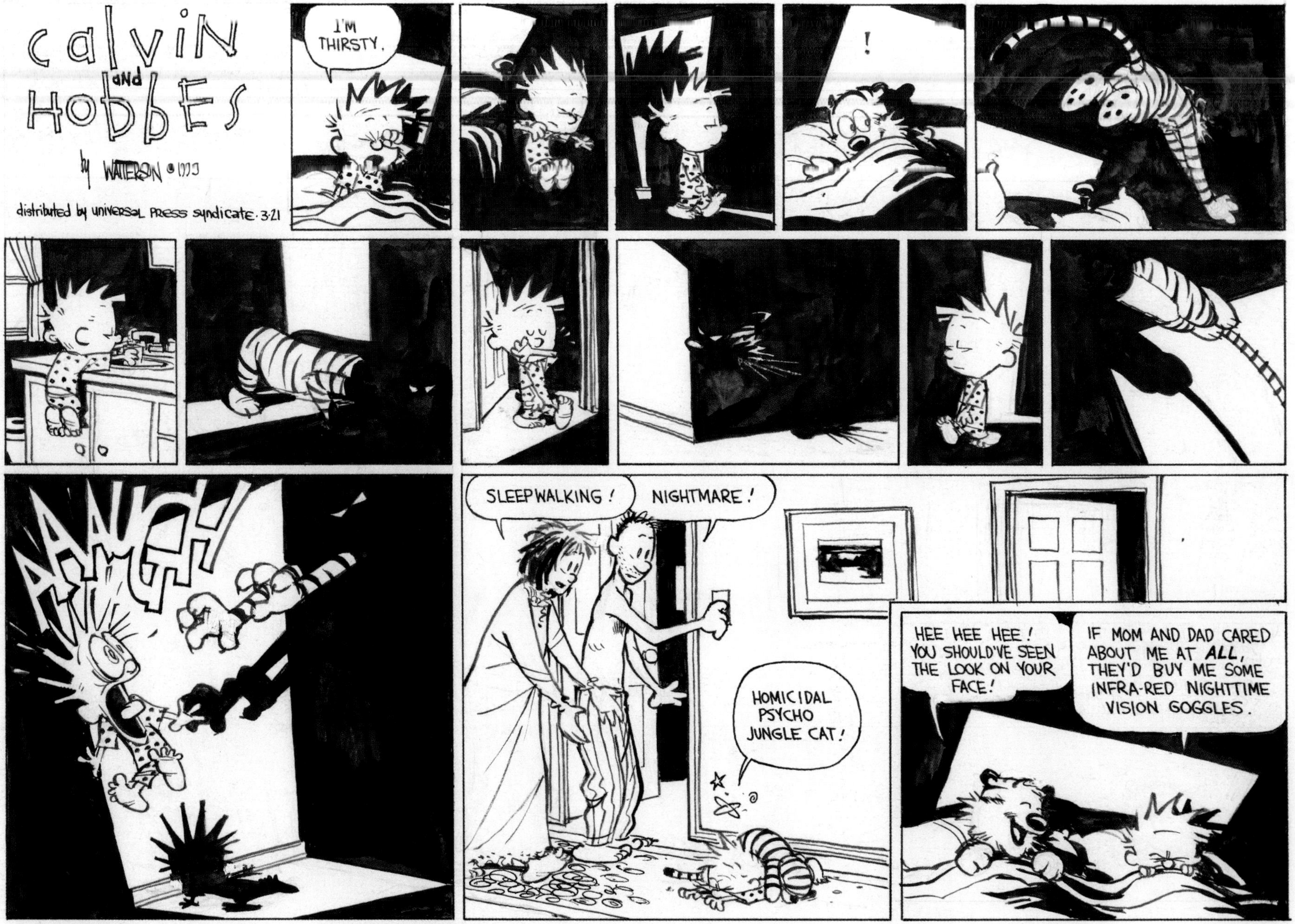
Calvin and Hobbes
by WATTERSON © 1993
distributed by universal press syndicate 3·21
I'M THIRSTY.
!
AAAUGH!
SLEEPWALKING!
NIGHTMARE!
HOMICIDAL PSYCHO JUNGLE CAT!
HEE HEE HEE! YOU SHOULD'VE SEEN THE LOOK ON YOUR FACE!
IF MOM AND DAD CARED ABOUT ME AT **ALL**, THEY'D BUY ME SOME INFRA-RED NIGHTTIME VISION GOGGLES.

MARCH 21, 1993

I can't read this strip without thinking of the cat who inspired much of Hobbes's personality. Sprite was an exuberant gray tabby we had. Enlarge her to tiger size, and this is what things would be like. The last panel drawing looks just like her.

This strip gave me my favorite book title.

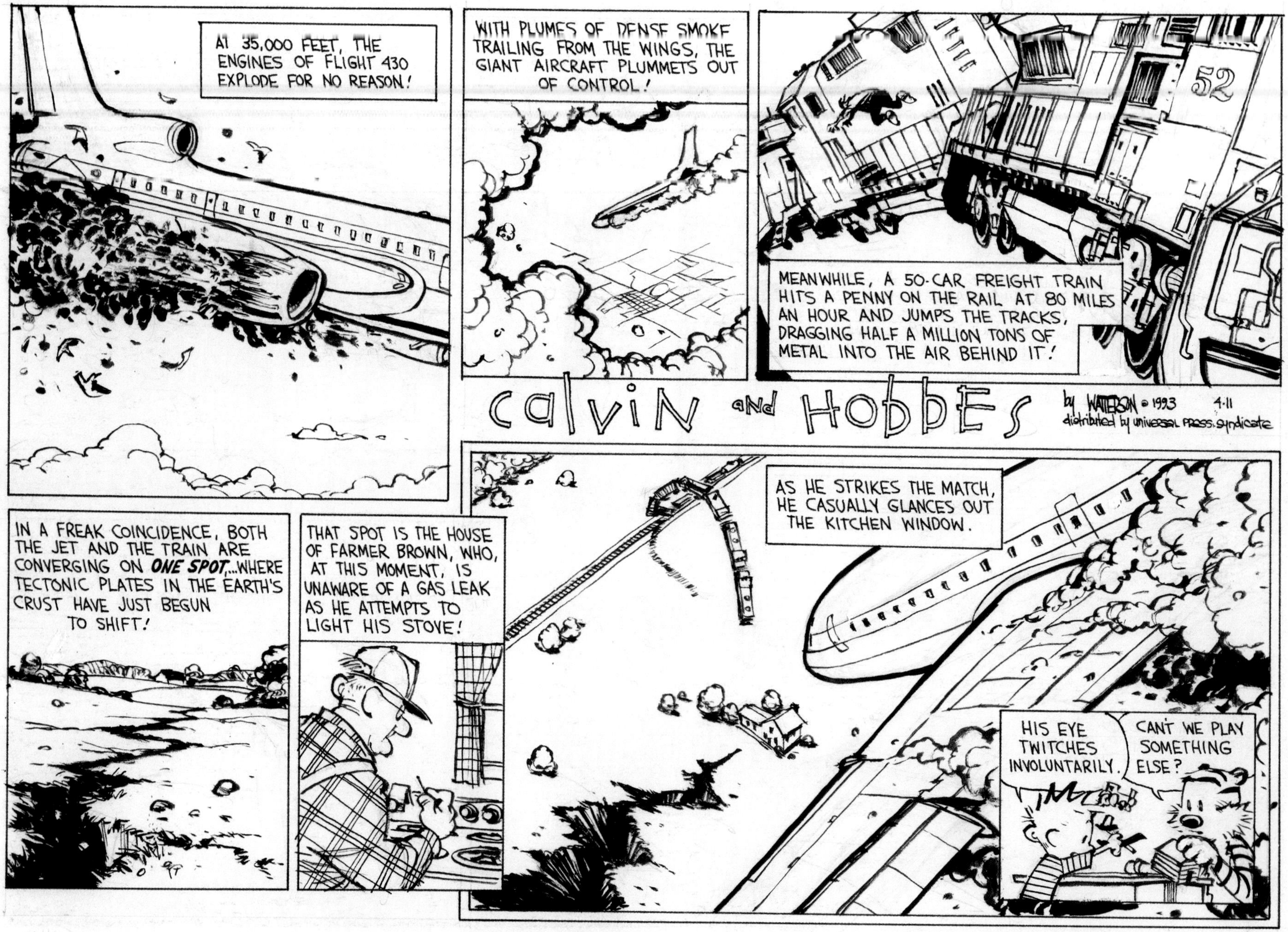
AT 35,000 FEET, THE ENGINES OF FLIGHT 430 EXPLODE FOR NO REASON!
WITH PLUMES OF DENSE SMOKE TRAILING FROM THE WINGS, THE GIANT AIRCRAFT PLUMMETS OUT OF CONTROL!
52
MEANWHILE, A 50-CAR FREIGHT TRAIN HITS A PENNY ON THE RAIL AT 80 MILES AN HOUR AND JUMPS THE TRACKS, DRAGGING HALF A MILLION TONS OF METAL INTO THE AIR BEHIND IT!
CALVIN AND HOBBES
by WATTERSON © 1993 4-11
distributed by universal press syndicate
IN A FREAK COINCIDENCE, BOTH THE JET AND THE TRAIN ARE CONVERGING ON ONE SPOT...WHERE TECTONIC PLATES IN THE EARTH'S CRUST HAVE JUST BEGUN TO SHIFT!
THAT SPOT IS THE HOUSE OF FARMER BROWN, WHO, AT THIS MOMENT, IS UNAWARE OF A GAS LEAK AS HE ATTEMPTS TO LIGHT HIS STOVE!
AS HE STRIKES THE MATCH, HE CASUALLY GLANCES OUT THE KITCHEN WINDOW.
HIS EYE TWITCHES INVOLUNTARILY.
CAN'T WE PLAY SOMETHING ELSE?

APRIL 11, 1993

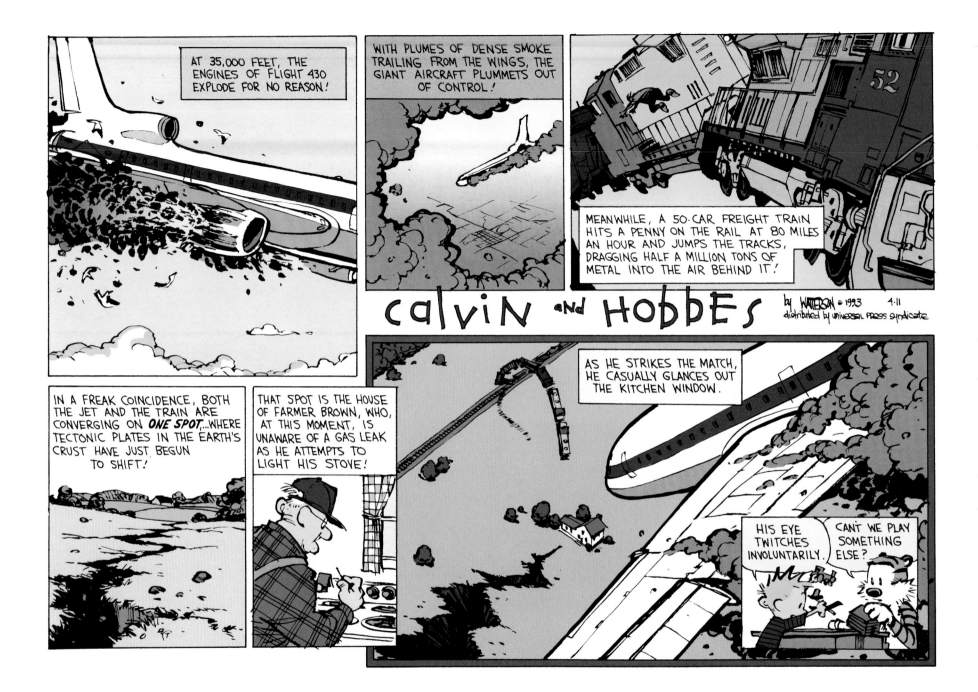

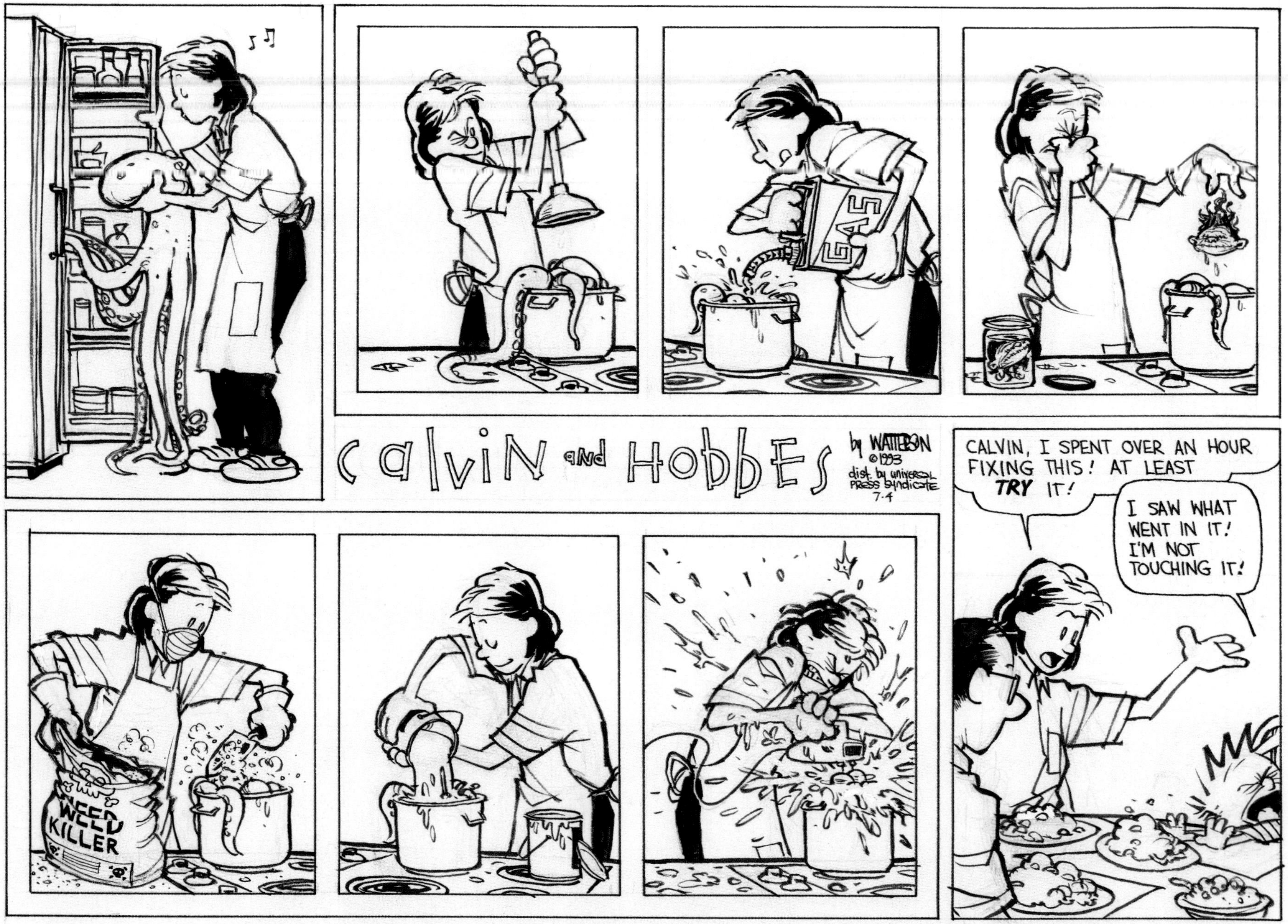
Calvin and Hobbes
by WATTERSON
©1993
dist. by universal press syndicate
7-4
GAS
WEED KILLER
CALVIN, I SPENT OVER AN HOUR FIXING THIS! AT LEAST TRY IT!
I SAW WHAT WENT IN IT! I'M NOT TOUCHING IT!

JULY 4, 1993

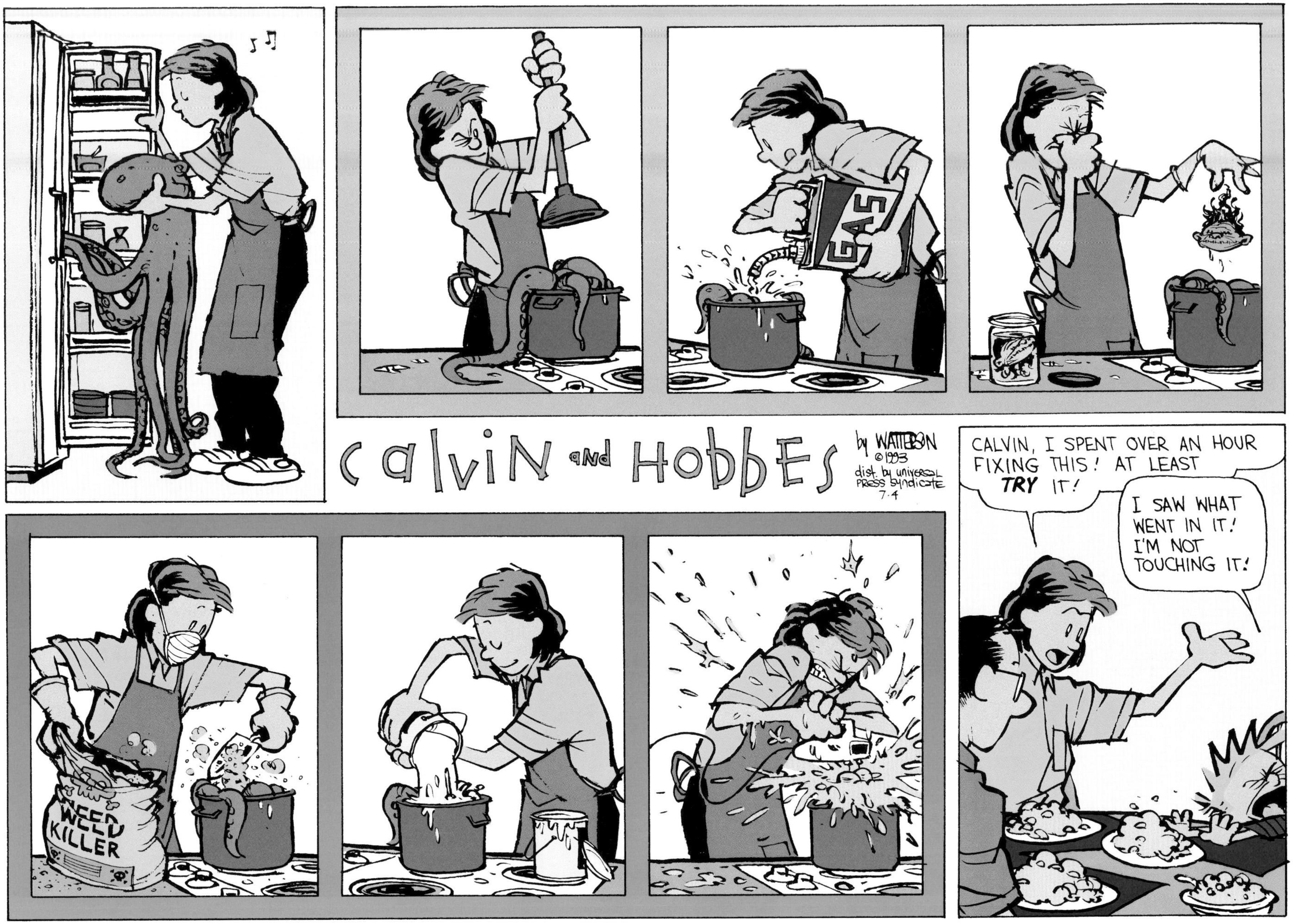
Calvin and Hobbes
by WATTERSON
©1993
dist. by universal press syndicate
7-4
GAS
CALVIN, I SPENT OVER AN HOUR FIXING THIS! AT LEAST TRY IT!
I SAW WHAT WENT IN IT! I'M NOT TOUCHING IT!
WEED KILLER

I like the little touches in these drawings—the octopus legs trailing out of the fridge, the use of a plumber's helper as a cooking utensil, the notion that shrunken heads might be sold in jars, etc. As you might guess, I was an unappreciative little kid once.

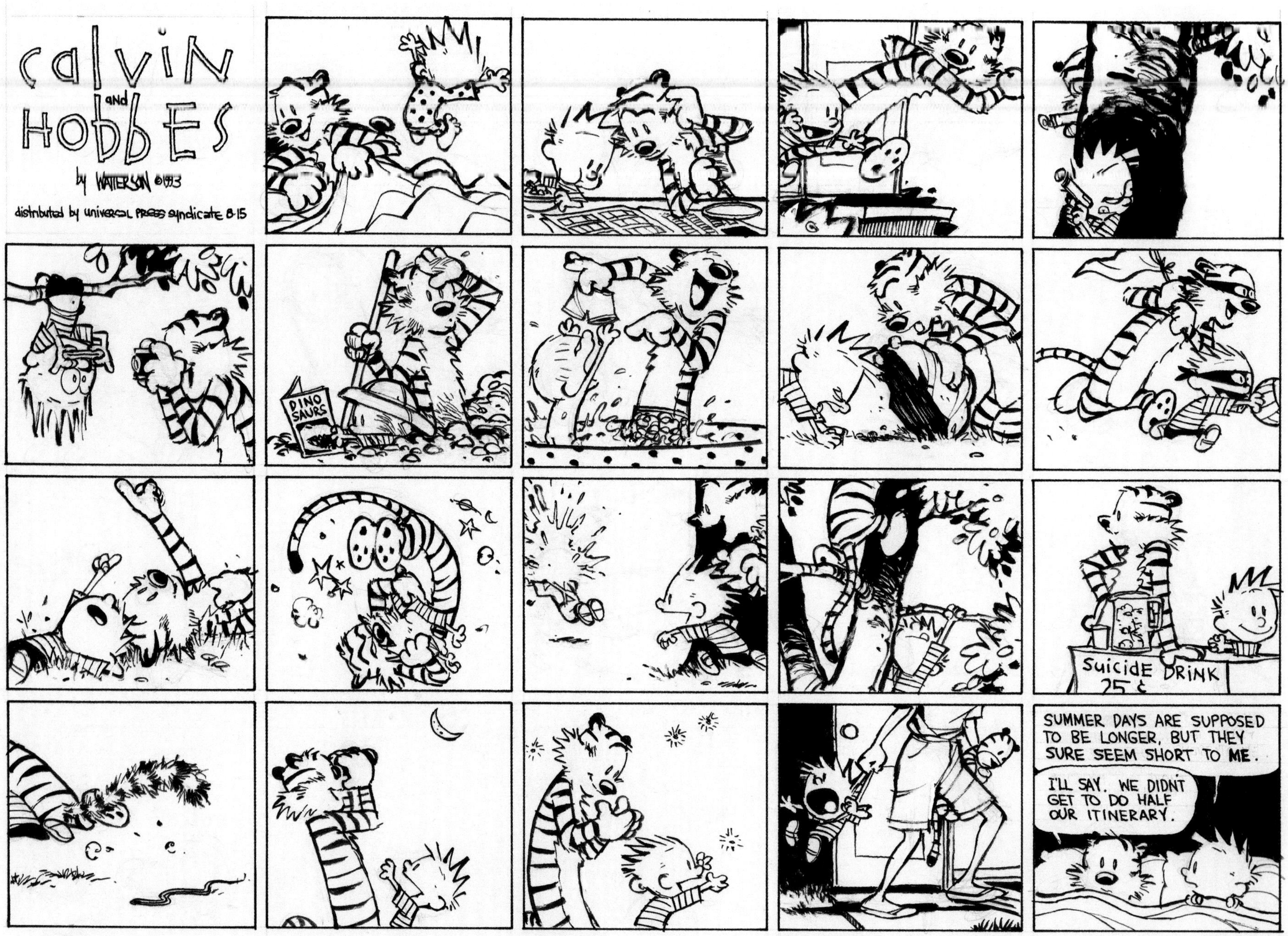
Calvin and Hobbes
by WATTERSON ©1993
distributed by universal press syndicate 8-15
DINO SAURS
SUICIDE DRINK 25¢
SUMMER DAYS ARE SUPPOSED TO BE LONGER, BUT THEY SURE SEEM SHORT TO **ME**.
I'LL SAY. WE DIDN'T GET TO DO HALF OUR ITINERARY.

August 15, 1993

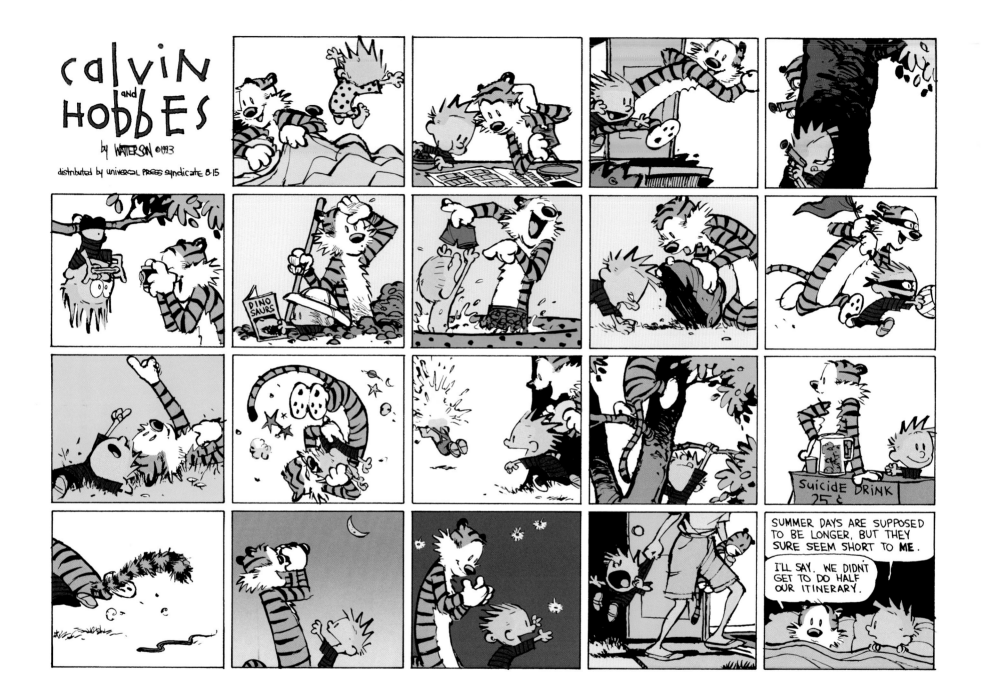

Count 'em: nineteen panels. You can draw a big, fat summer day in nineteen panels. This strip would have a very different feel with less space.

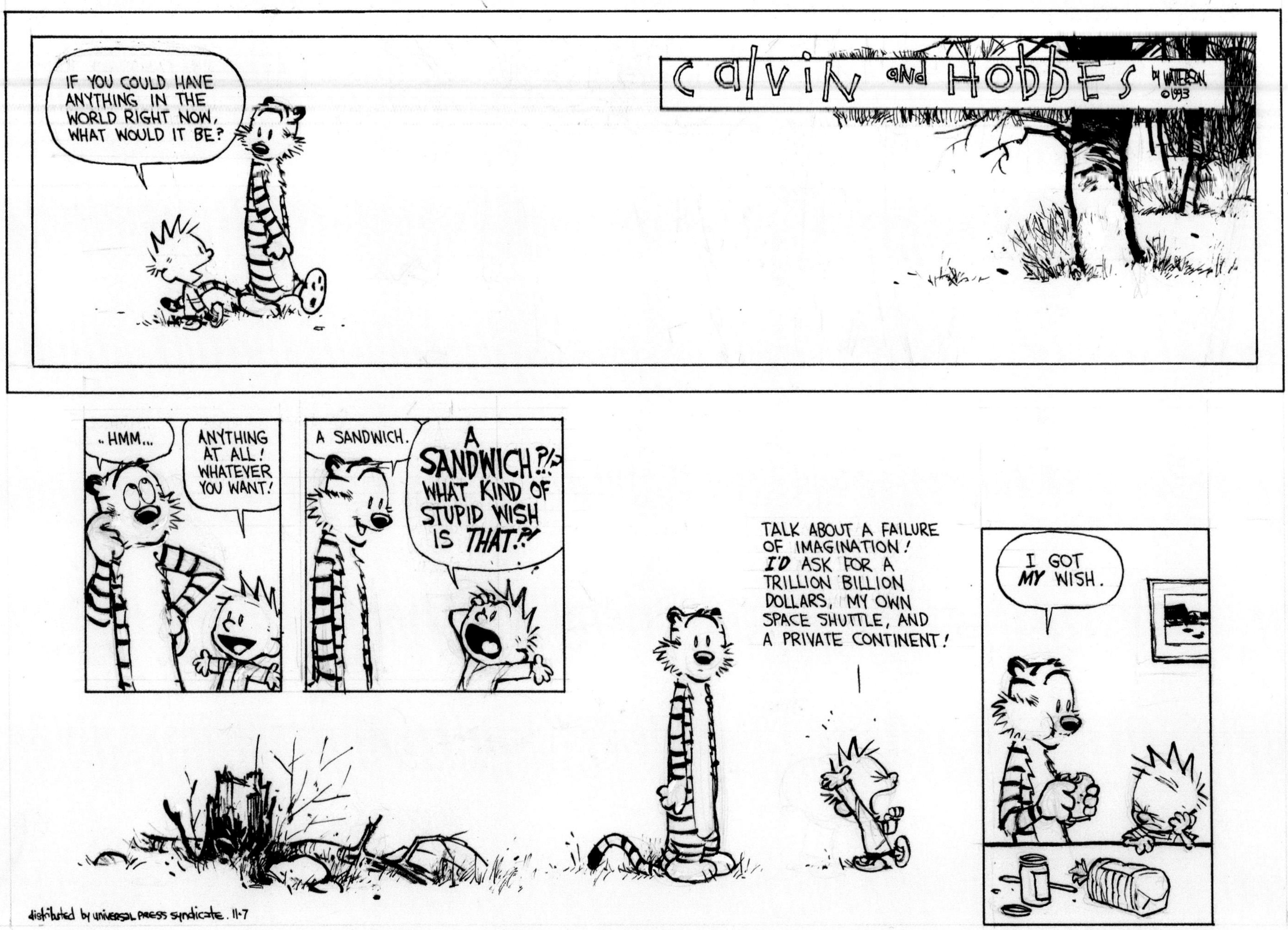
Calvin and HOBBES by WATTERSON ©1993
IF YOU COULD HAVE ANYTHING IN THE WORLD RIGHT NOW, WHAT WOULD IT BE?
..HMM...
ANYTHING AT ALL! WHATEVER YOU WANT!
A SANDWICH.
A SANDWICH?!? WHAT KIND OF STUPID WISH IS THAT?!
TALK ABOUT A FAILURE OF IMAGINATION! I'D ASK FOR A TRILLION BILLION DOLLARS, MY OWN SPACE SHUTTLE, AND A PRIVATE CONTINENT!
I GOT MY WISH.
distributed by universal press syndicate. 11-7

NOVEMBER 7, 1993

I sometimes tried for the spare visual effect of a Japanese print—very few things, but precisely placed. In November strips, I always tried to capture that austere, gray, brambly look that Ohio gets.

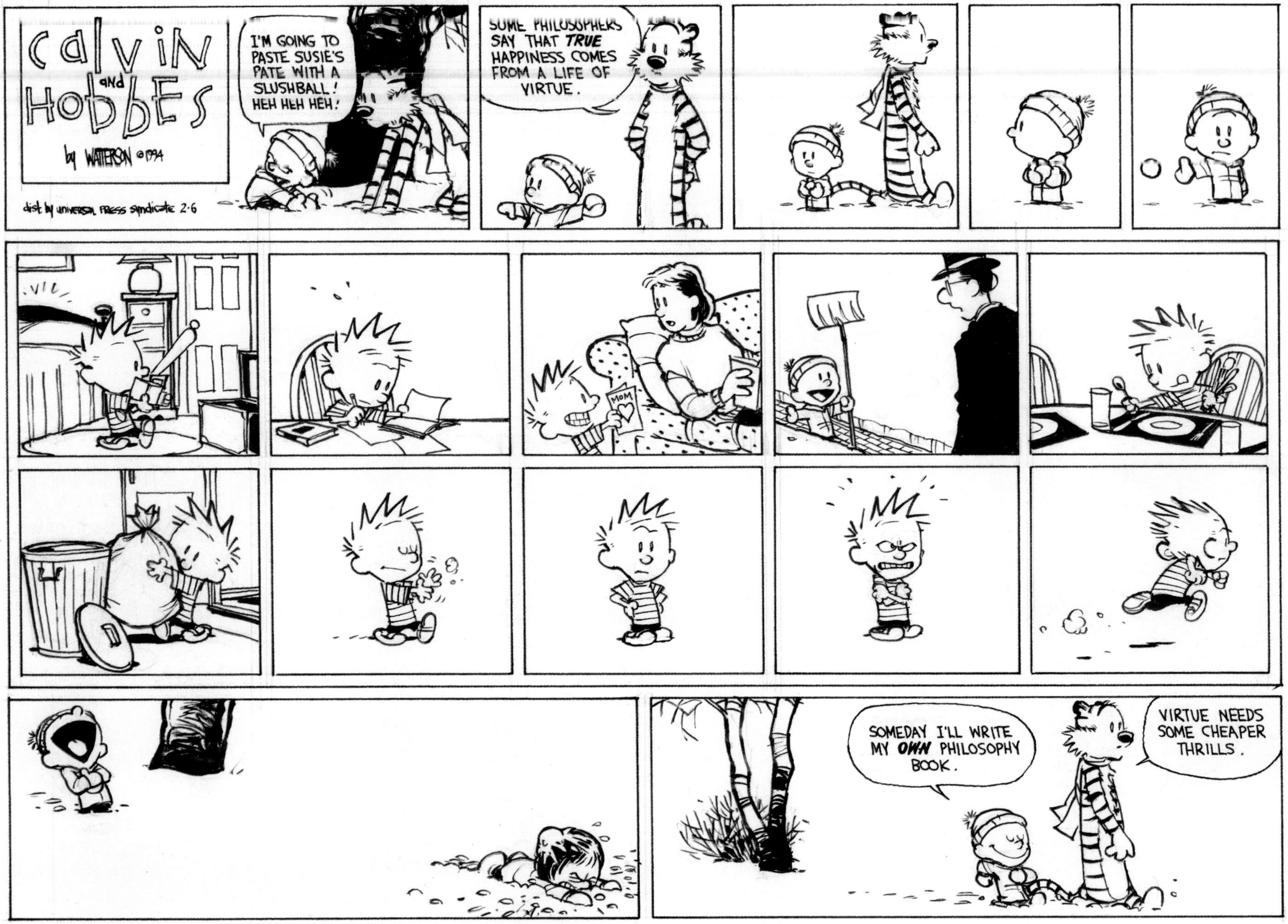
Calvin and Hobbes
by WATTERSON ©1994
dist. by Universal Press Syndicate 2·6
I'M GOING TO PASTE SUSIE'S PATE WITH A SLUSHBALL! HEH HEH HEH!
SOME PHILOSOPHERS SAY THAT TRUE HAPPINESS COMES FROM A LIFE OF VIRTUE.
MOM
SOMEDAY I'LL WRITE MY OWN PHILOSOPHY BOOK.
VIRTUE NEEDS SOME CHEAPER THRILLS.

FEBRUARY 6, 1994

The choice between good and evil was a recurring theme in the strip, and nothing tested Calvin like a good slushball.

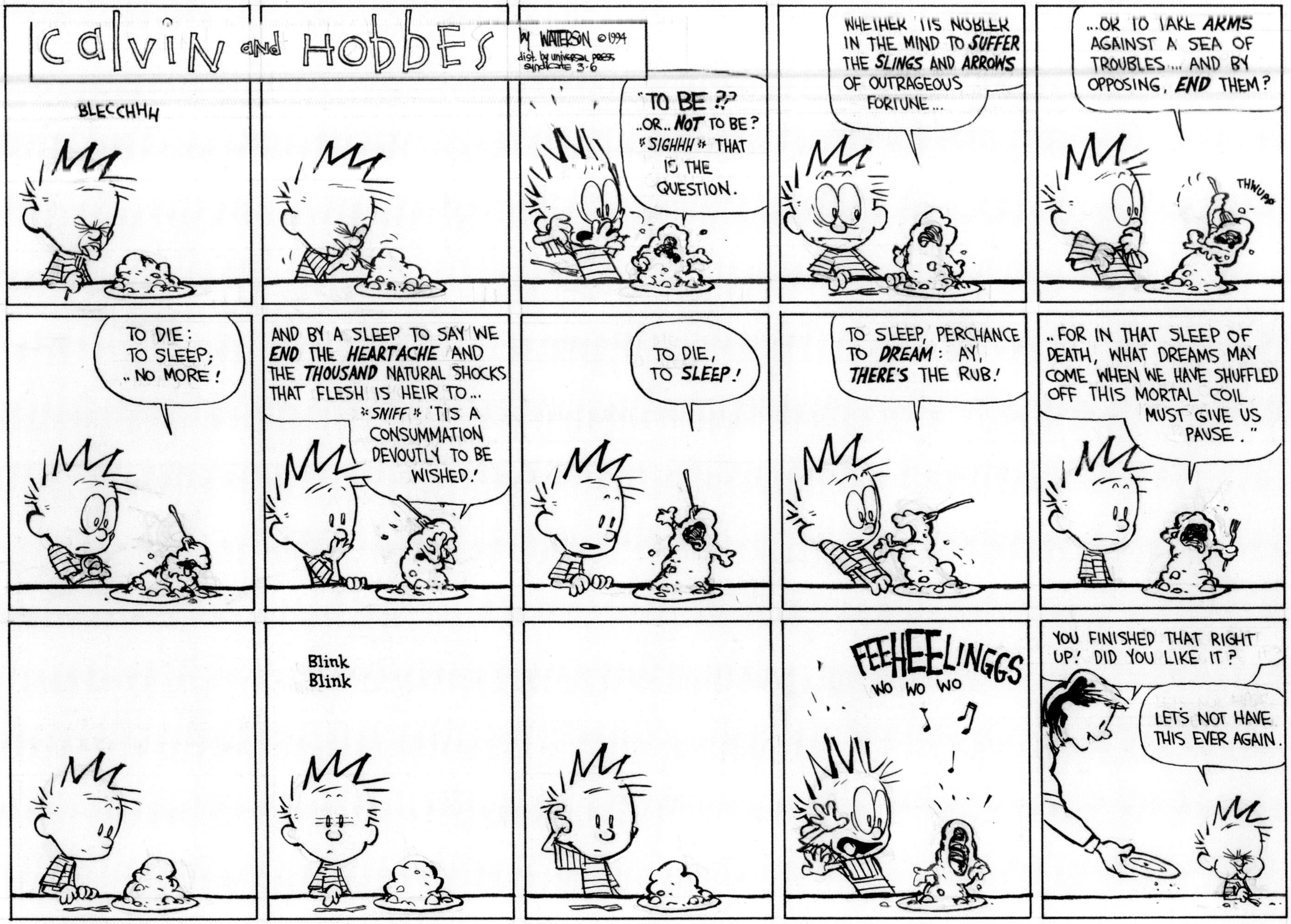
Calvin and Hobbes
by WATTERSON © 1994
dist. by Universal Press Syndicate 3-6
BLECCHHH
TO BE ?!?
..OR.. NOT TO BE?
SIGHHH THAT IS THE QUESTION.
WHETHER 'TIS NOBLER IN THE MIND TO SUFFER THE SLINGS AND ARROWS OF OUTRAGEOUS FORTUNE...
...OR TO TAKE ARMS AGAINST A SEA OF TROUBLES... AND BY OPPOSING, END THEM?
THWUPP
TO DIE: TO SLEEP; ..NO MORE!
AND BY A SLEEP TO SAY WE END THE HEARTACHE AND THE THOUSAND NATURAL SHOCKS THAT FLESH IS HEIR TO...
SNIFF 'TIS A CONSUMMATION DEVOUTLY TO BE WISHED!
TO DIE, TO SLEEP!
TO SLEEP, PERCHANCE TO DREAM: AY, THERE'S THE RUB!
..FOR IN THAT SLEEP OF DEATH, WHAT DREAMS MAY COME WHEN WE HAVE SHUFFLED OFF THIS MORTAL COIL MUST GIVE US PAUSE."
Blink
Blink
FEEHEELINGGS
WO WO WO
YOU FINISHED THAT RIGHT UP! DID YOU LIKE IT?
LET'S NOT HAVE THIS EVER AGAIN.

MARCH 6, 1994

This is one of the weirdest strips I drew, and I'm not exactly sure I understand it myself, but it still makes me laugh, so there you are.

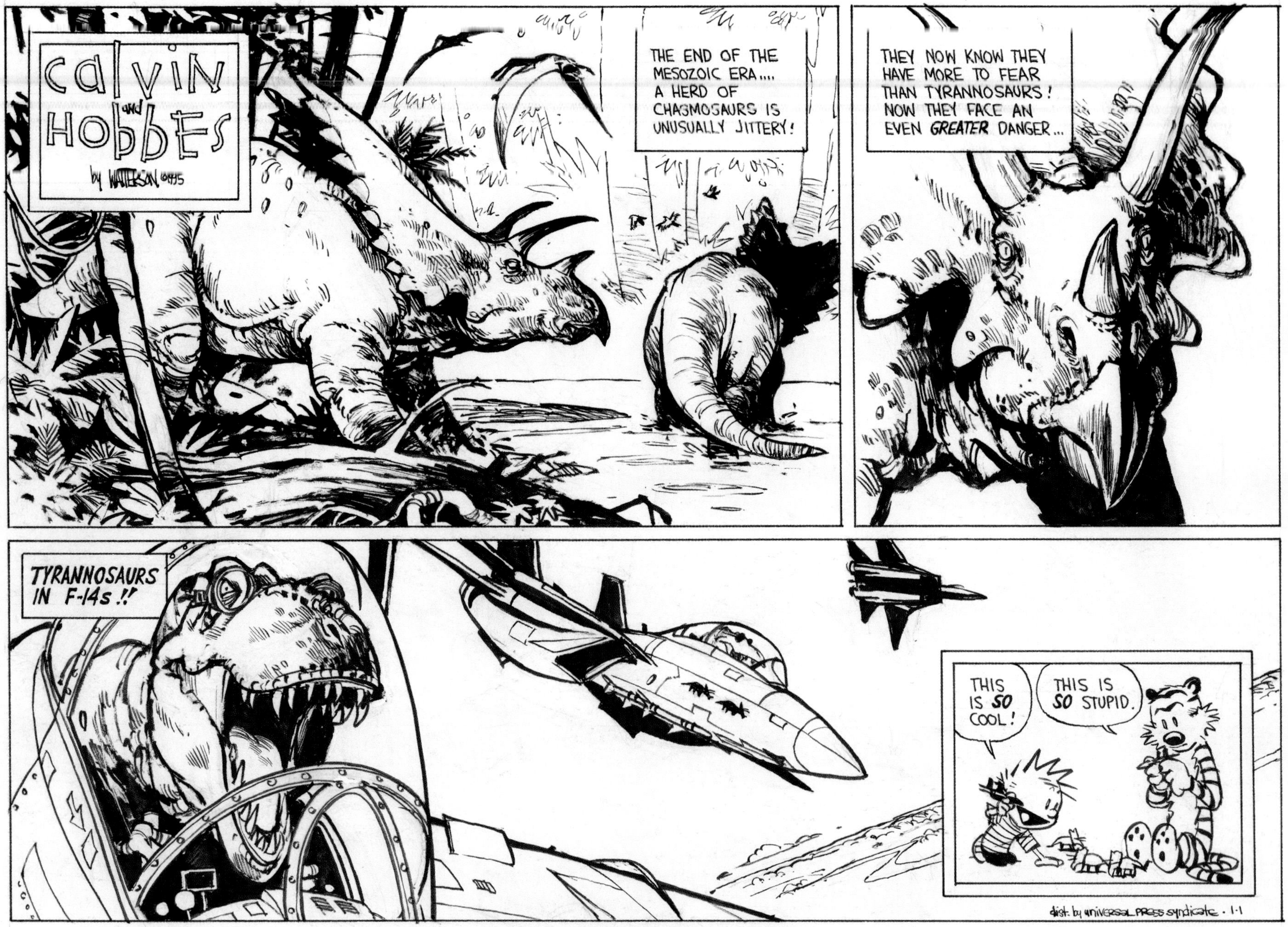
Calvin and Hobbes
by WATTERSON ©1995
THE END OF THE MESOZOIC ERA.... A HERD OF CHASMOSAURS IS UNUSUALLY JITTERY!
THEY NOW KNOW THEY HAVE MORE TO FEAR THAN TYRANNOSAURS! NOW THEY FACE AN EVEN GREATER DANGER...
TYRANNOSAURS IN F-14s!!
THIS IS SO COOL!
THIS IS SO STUPID.
dist. by universal press syndicate · 1·1

January 1, 1995

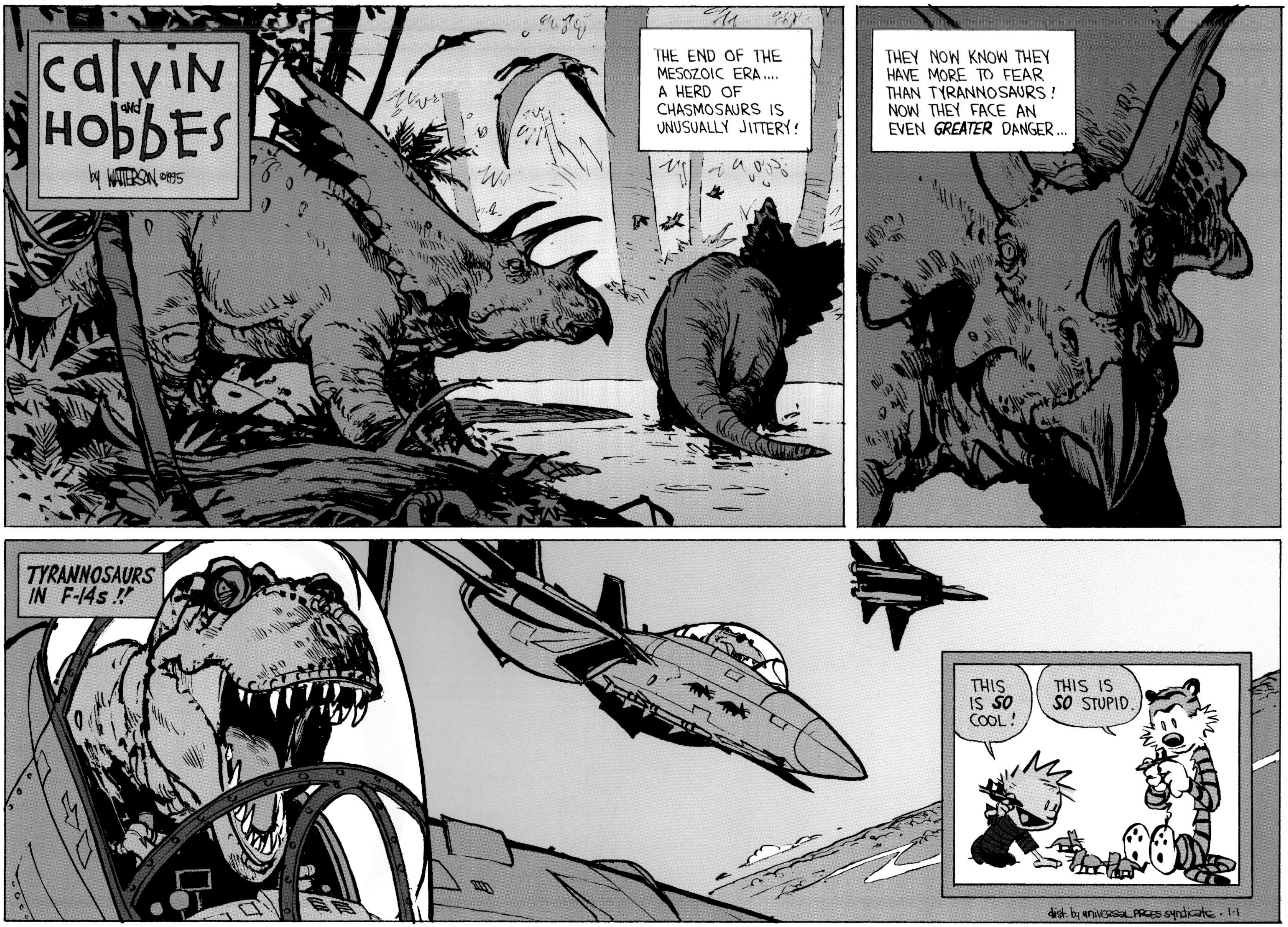
Calvin and Hobbes
by WATTERSON ©1995
THE END OF THE MESOZOIC ERA.... A HERD OF CHASMOSAURS IS UNUSUALLY JITTERY!
THEY NOW KNOW THEY HAVE MORE TO FEAR THAN TYRANNOSAURS! NOW THEY FACE AN EVEN GREATER DANGER...
TYRANNOSAURS IN F-14s!!
THIS IS SO COOL!
THIS IS SO STUPID.
dist. by universal press syndicate · 1-1

The dinosaur strips always took forever to draw, since I had to imagine and construct them from skeleton diagrams and other illustrations. They were a lot of fun if the deadlines weren't right on top of me. This one was a little tricky, because the T. Rex anatomy doesn't fit easily into an airplane cockpit, and it required a little fudging.

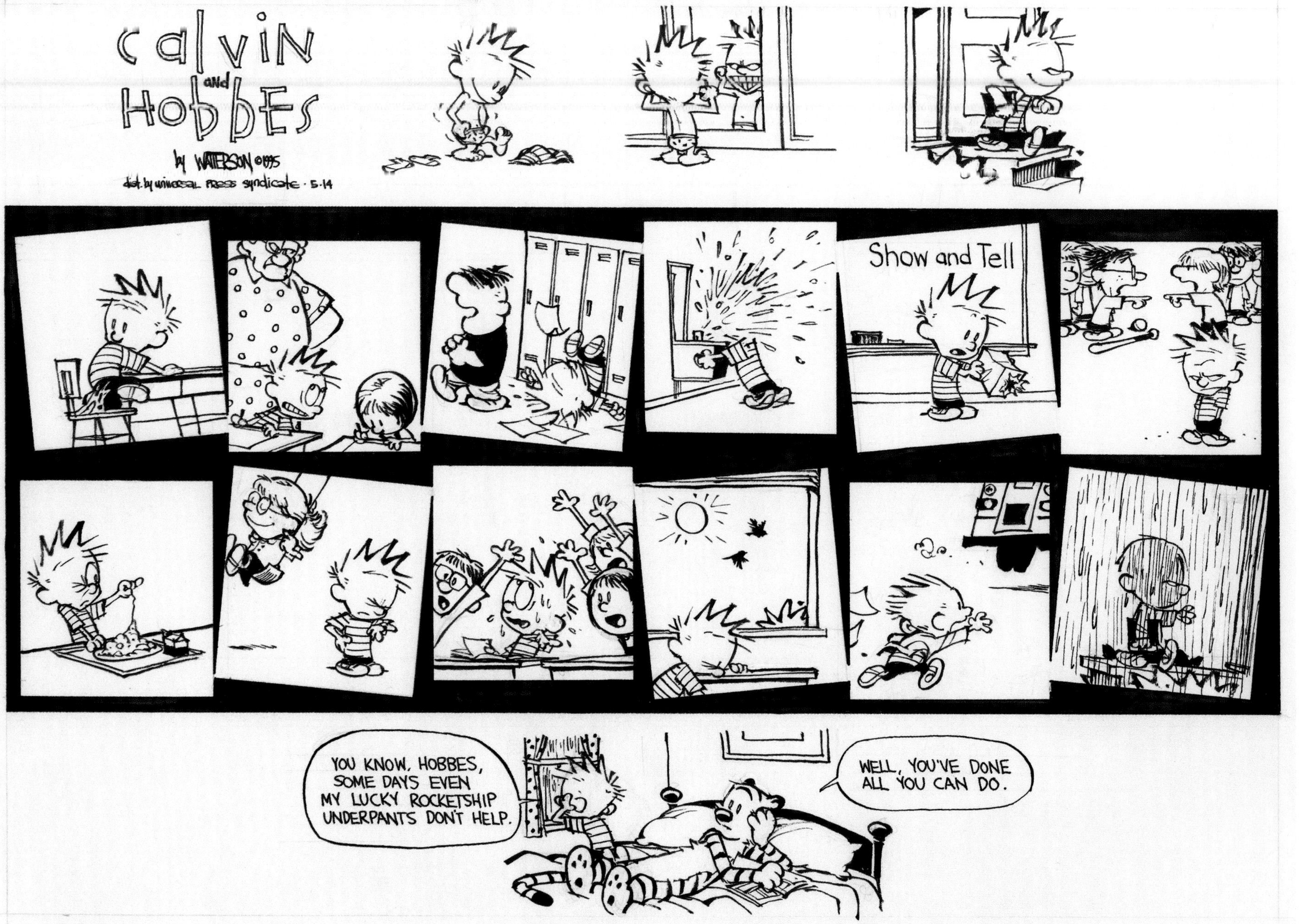
Calvin and Hobbes
by WATTERSON ©1995
dist. by universal press syndicate · 5-14
Show and Tell
YOU KNOW, HOBBES, SOME DAYS EVEN MY LUCKY ROCKETSHIP UNDERPANTS DON'T HELP.
WELL, YOU'VE DONE ALL YOU CAN DO.

MAY 14, 1995

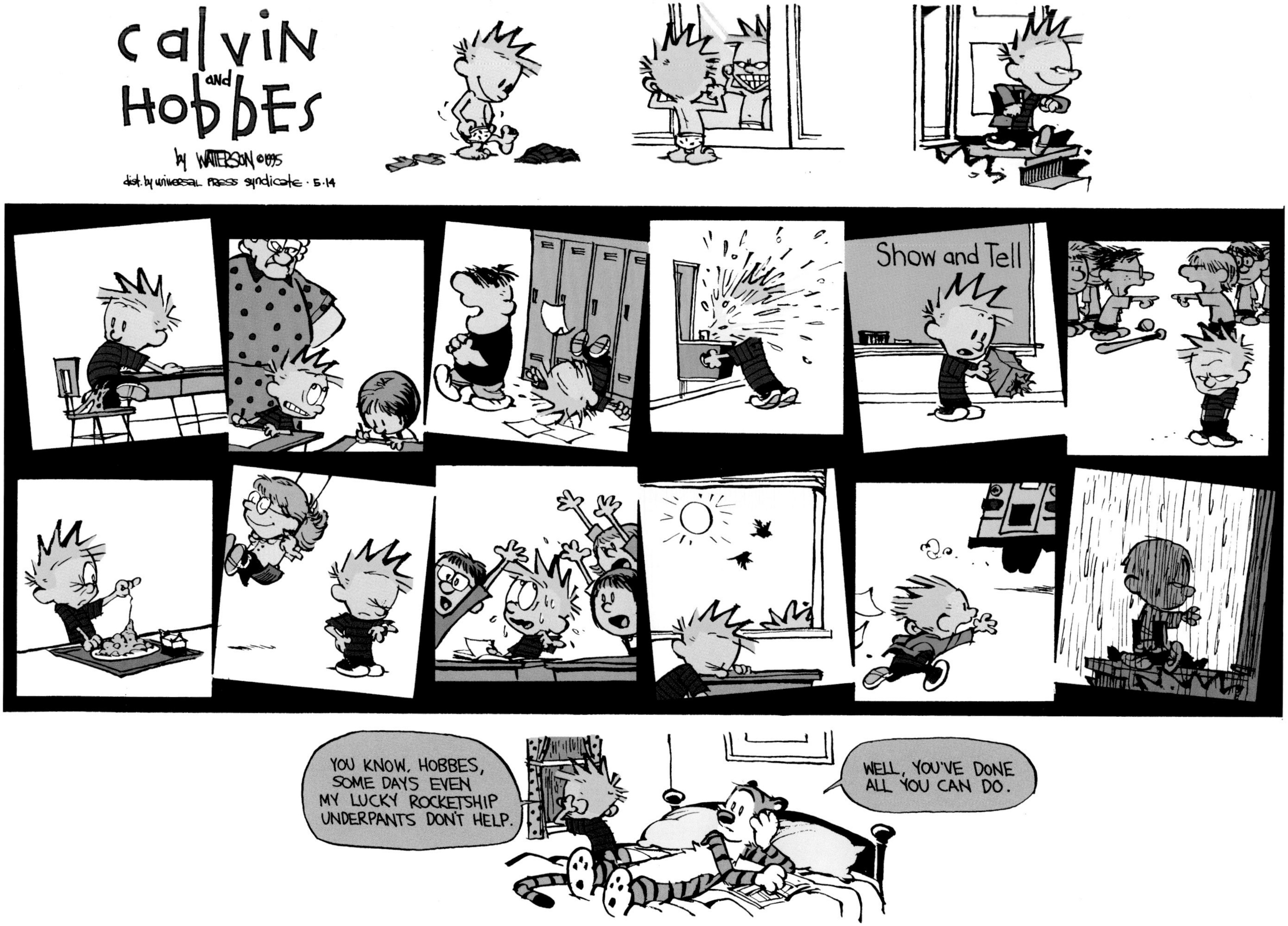
Calvin and Hobbes
by WATTERSON ©1995
dist. by universal press syndicate · 5·14
Show and Tell
YOU KNOW, HOBBES, SOME DAYS EVEN MY LUCKY ROCKETSHIP UNDERPANTS DON'T HELP.
WELL, YOU'VE DONE ALL YOU CAN DO.

If I had any extra room to spare, I'd try to make the panel design interesting. Here the large black rectangle visually separates Calvin's school day from his time at home. The crooked panels and heavy use of black are tricks I learned from *Krazy Kat*. This sort of design can be distracting and annoying if not handled with restraint. The panels can be interesting, but they should never divert attention from the drawings.

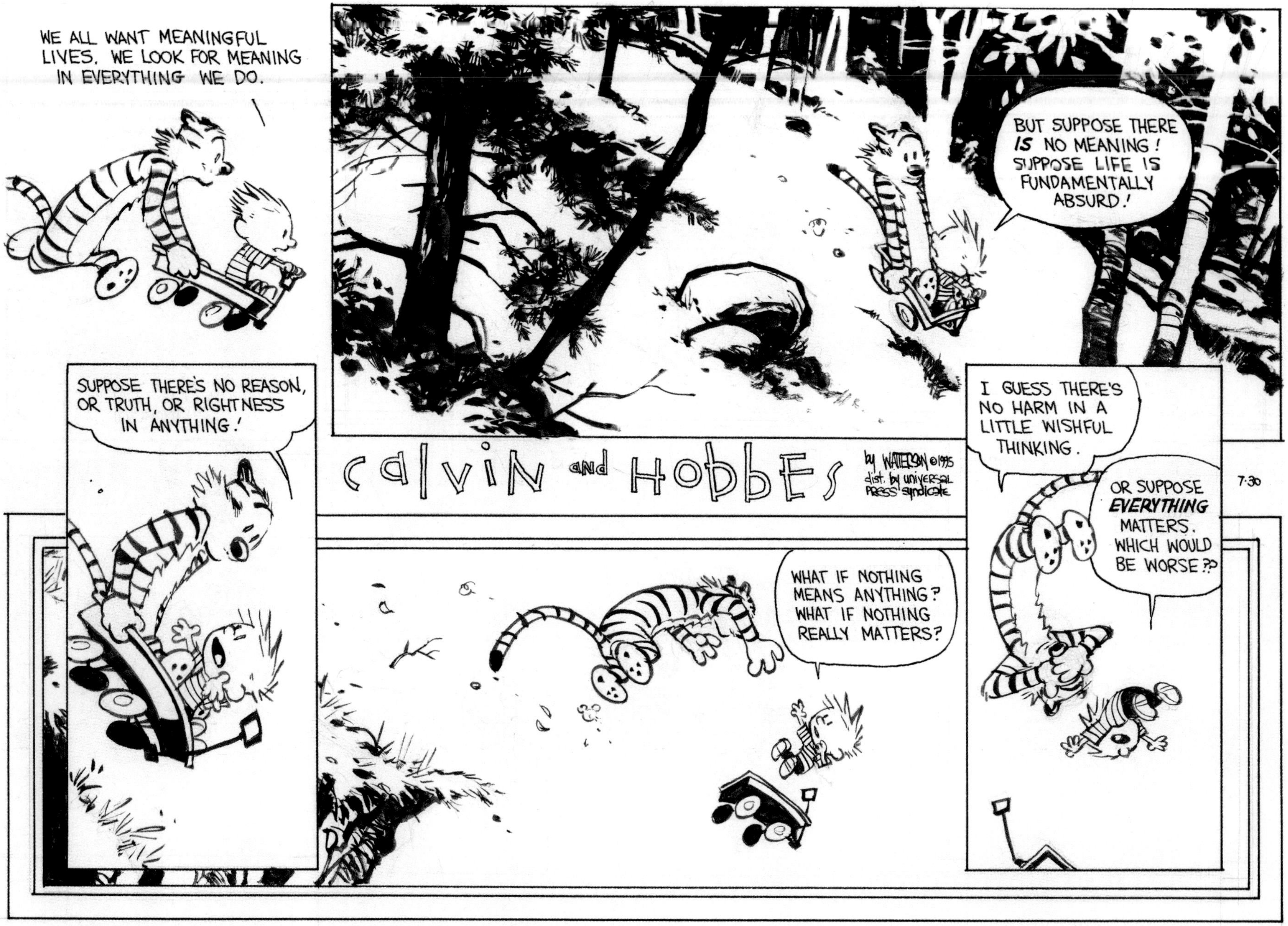
WE ALL WANT MEANINGFUL LIVES. WE LOOK FOR MEANING IN EVERYTHING WE DO.
BUT SUPPOSE THERE *IS* NO MEANING! SUPPOSE LIFE IS FUNDAMENTALLY ABSURD!
Calvin and HOBBES
by WATTERSON ©1995 dist. by universal press syndicate
SUPPOSE THERE'S NO REASON, OR TRUTH, OR RIGHTNESS IN ANYTHING!
WHAT IF NOTHING MEANS ANYTHING? WHAT IF NOTHING REALLY MATTERS?
I GUESS THERE'S NO HARM IN A LITTLE WISHFUL THINKING.
OR SUPPOSE *EVERYTHING* MATTERS. WHICH WOULD BE WORSE??
7·30

JULY 30, 1995

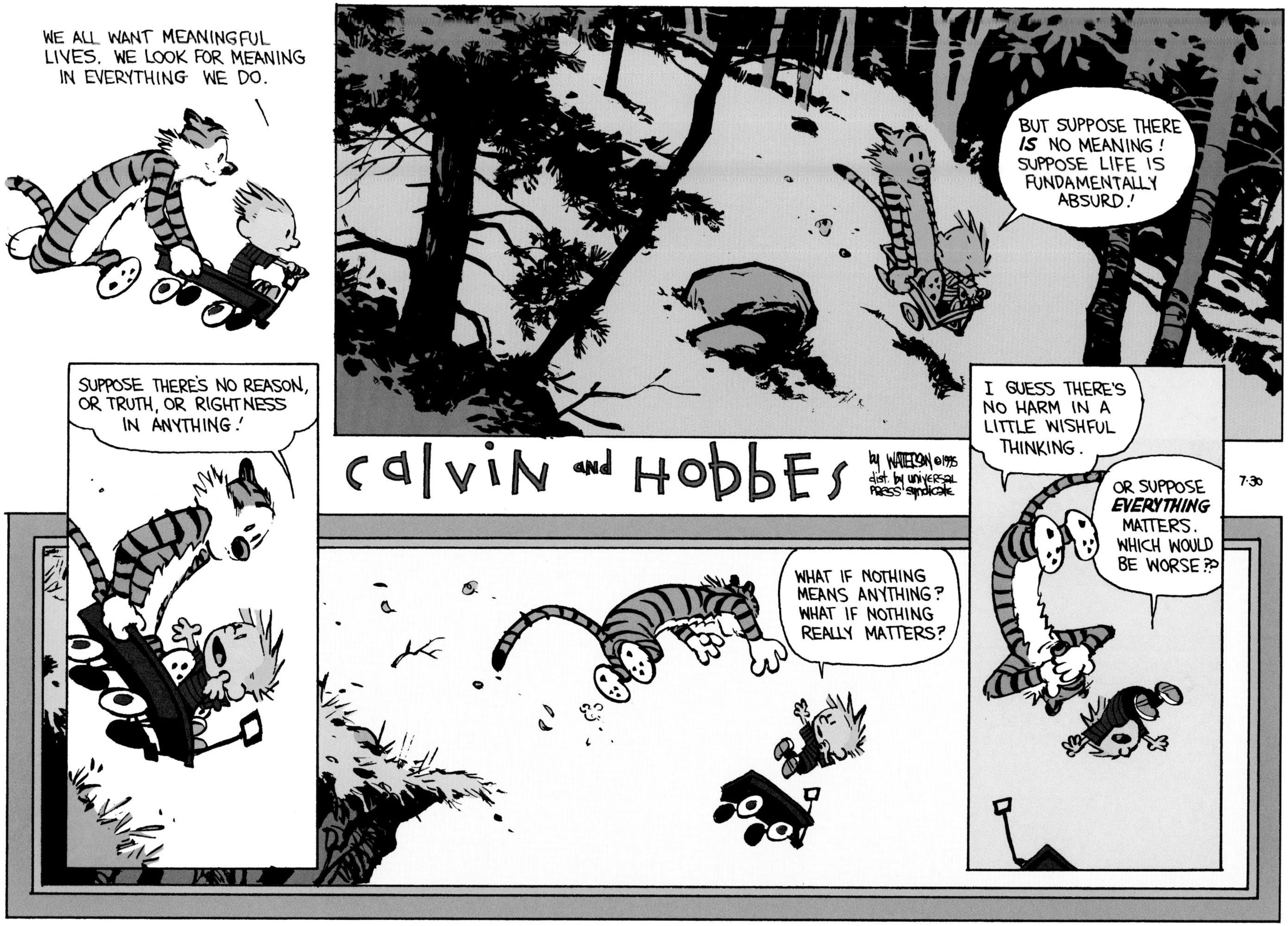
WE ALL WANT MEANINGFUL LIVES. WE LOOK FOR MEANING IN EVERYTHING WE DO.
BUT SUPPOSE THERE IS NO MEANING! SUPPOSE LIFE IS FUNDAMENTALLY ABSURD!
SUPPOSE THERE'S NO REASON, OR TRUTH, OR RIGHTNESS IN ANYTHING!
calvin and HOBBES
by WATTERSON ©1995 dist. by universal press syndicate
WHAT IF NOTHING MEANS ANYTHING? WHAT IF NOTHING REALLY MATTERS?
I GUESS THERE'S NO HARM IN A LITTLE WISHFUL THINKING.
OR SUPPOSE EVERYTHING MATTERS. WHICH WOULD BE WORSE?!
7·30

Whenever the strip got ponderous, I put Calvin and Hobbes in their wagon and sent them over a cliff. It had a nice way of undercutting the serious subjects, and it often doubled as a visual metaphor as well. Plus, it's a lot more fun to draw than a series of talking heads.

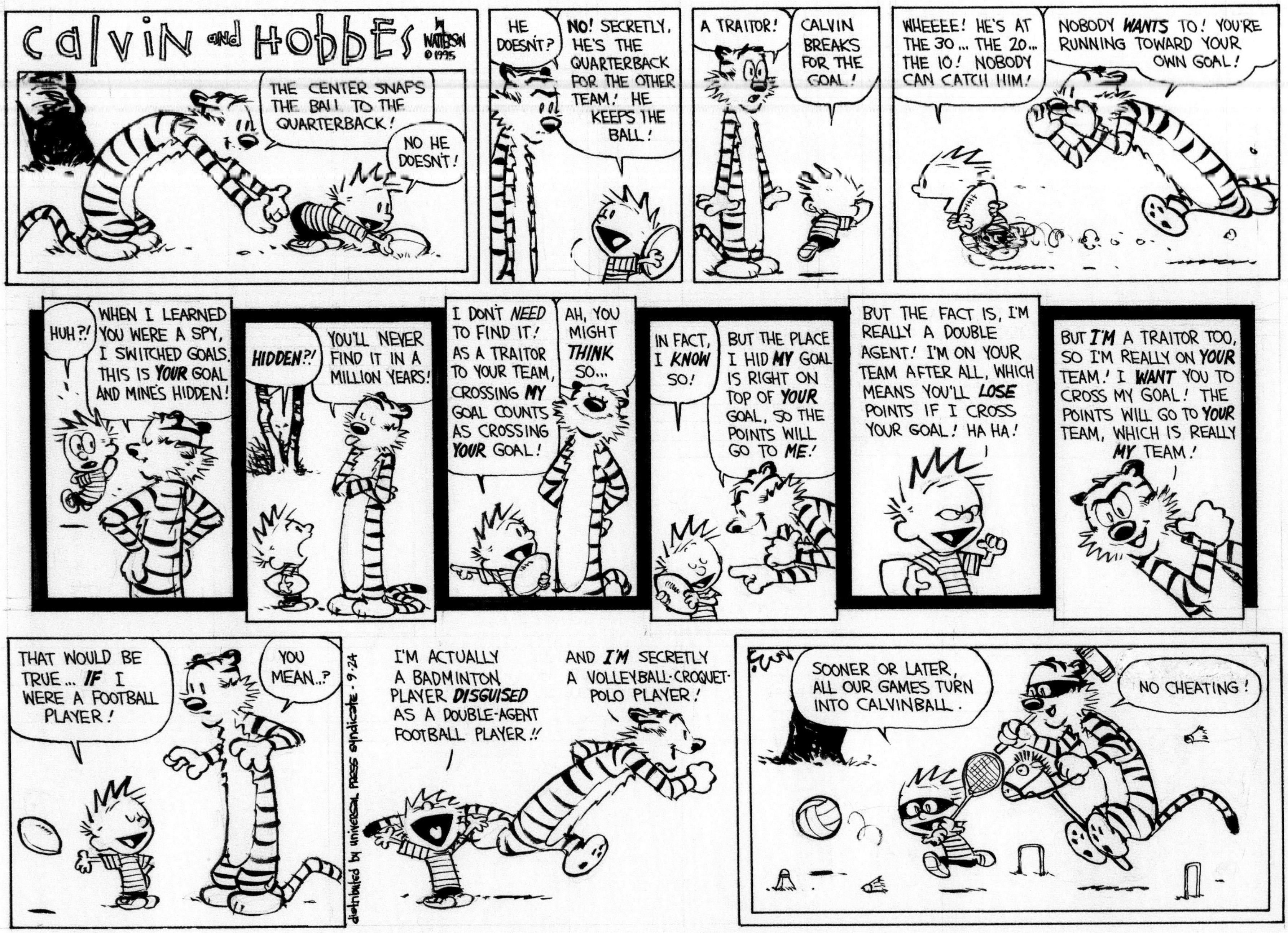
Calvin and Hobbes
by WATTERSON © 1995
THE CENTER SNAPS THE BALL TO THE QUARTERBACK!
NO HE DOESN'T!
HE DOESN'T?
NO! SECRETLY, HE'S THE QUARTERBACK FOR THE OTHER TEAM! HE KEEPS THE BALL!
A TRAITOR!
CALVIN BREAKS FOR THE GOAL!
WHEEEE! HE'S AT THE 30... THE 20... THE 10! NOBODY CAN CATCH HIM!
NOBODY WANTS TO! YOU'RE RUNNING TOWARD YOUR OWN GOAL!
HUH?!
WHEN I LEARNED YOU WERE A SPY, I SWITCHED GOALS. THIS IS YOUR GOAL AND MINE'S HIDDEN!
HIDDEN?!
YOU'LL NEVER FIND IT IN A MILLION YEARS!
I DON'T NEED TO FIND IT! AS A TRAITOR TO YOUR TEAM, CROSSING MY GOAL COUNTS AS CROSSING YOUR GOAL!
AH, YOU MIGHT THINK SO...
IN FACT, I KNOW SO!
BUT THE PLACE I HID MY GOAL IS RIGHT ON TOP OF YOUR GOAL, SO THE POINTS WILL GO TO ME!
BUT THE FACT IS, I'M REALLY A DOUBLE AGENT! I'M ON YOUR TEAM AFTER ALL, WHICH MEANS YOU'LL LOSE POINTS IF I CROSS YOUR GOAL! HA HA!
BUT I'M A TRAITOR TOO, SO I'M REALLY ON YOUR TEAM! I WANT YOU TO CROSS MY GOAL! THE POINTS WILL GO TO YOUR TEAM, WHICH IS REALLY MY TEAM!
THAT WOULD BE TRUE... IF I WERE A FOOTBALL PLAYER!
YOU MEAN..?
distributed by Universal Press Syndicate · 9-24
I'M ACTUALLY A BADMINTON PLAYER DISGUISED AS A DOUBLE-AGENT FOOTBALL PLAYER!!
AND I'M SECRETLY A VOLLEYBALL-CROQUET-POLO PLAYER!
SOONER OR LATER, ALL OUR GAMES TURN INTO CALVINBALL.
NO CHEATING!

SEPTEMBER 24, 1995

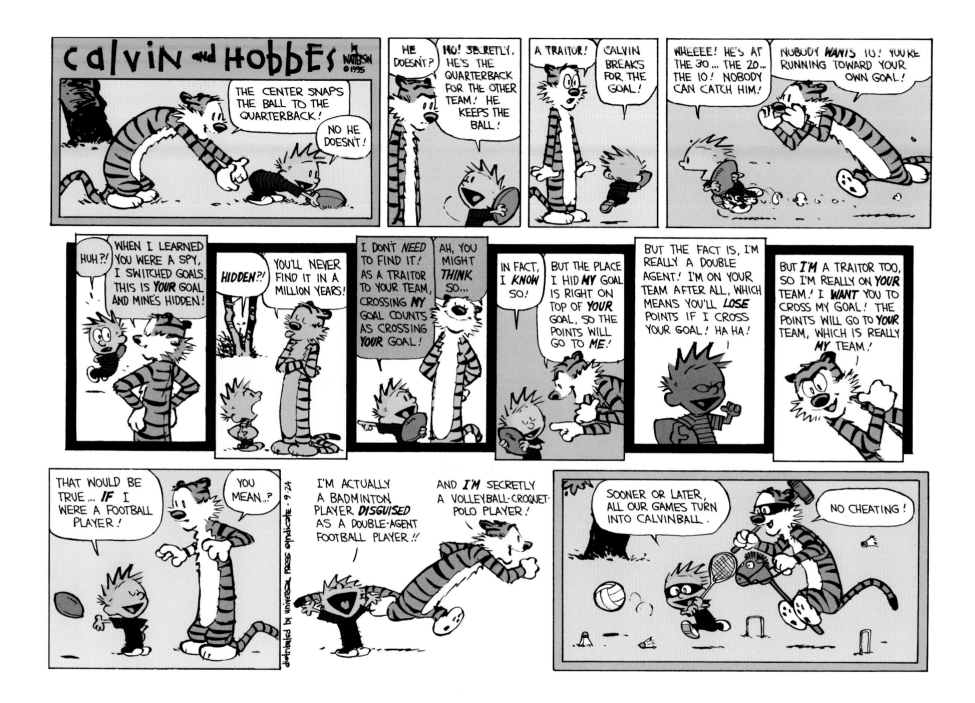

This strip has a lot of back and forth conversation, and the idea was to create a sense of escalating lunacy. Once again, you can't do this sort of thing in just a few panels. Nor would this work across several daily strips—you'd lose the momentum. The large Sunday format captured the spirit of *Calvin and Hobbes* in ways that had been impossible before.

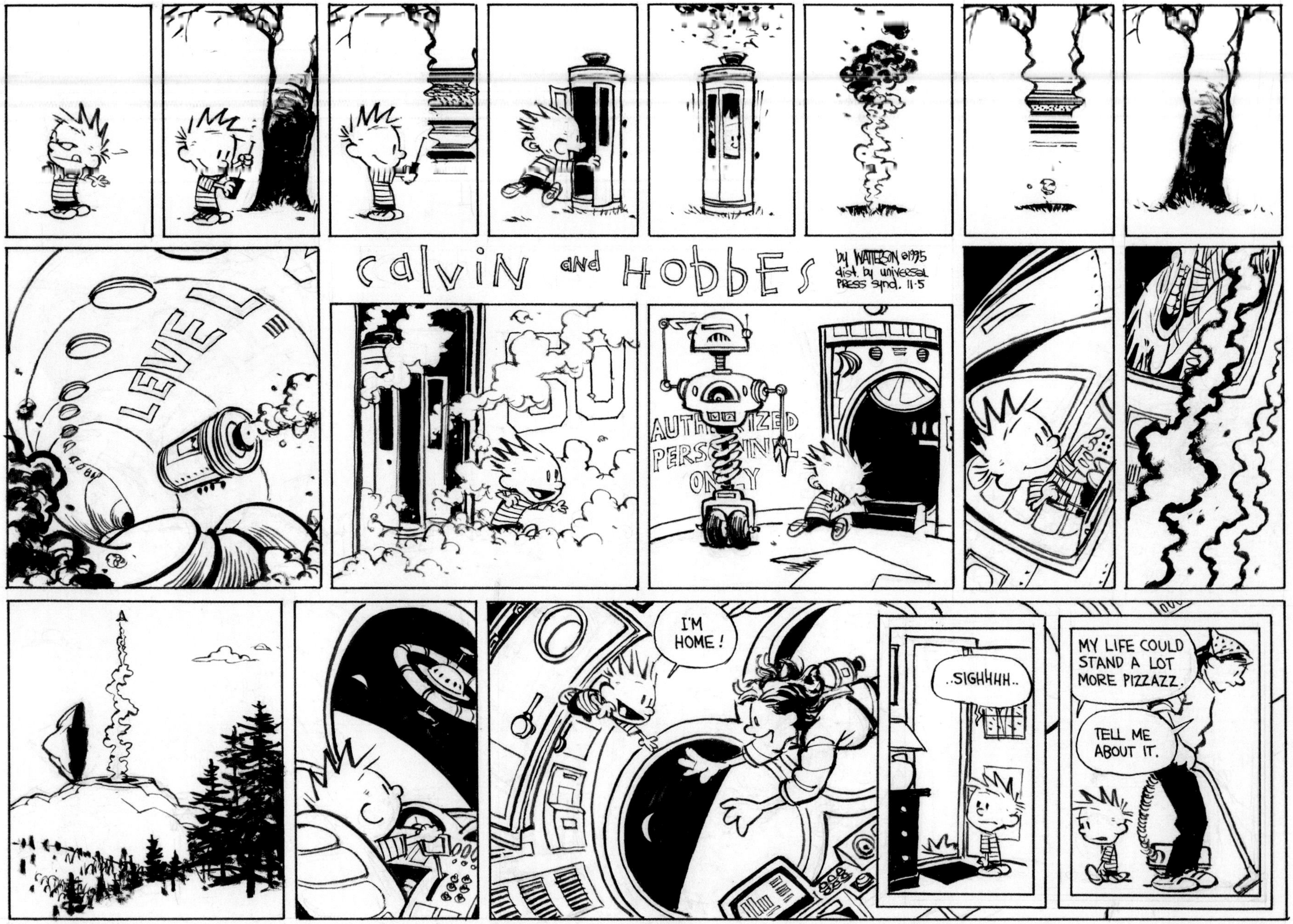

Calvin and HOBBES
by WATTERSON ©1995 dist. by universal PRESS synd. 11·5
LEVEL
AUTH ZED PERS NEL ON Y
I'M HOME!
..SIGHHHH..
MY LIFE COULD STAND A LOT MORE PIZZAZZ.
TELL ME ABOUT IT.

NOVEMBER 5, 1995

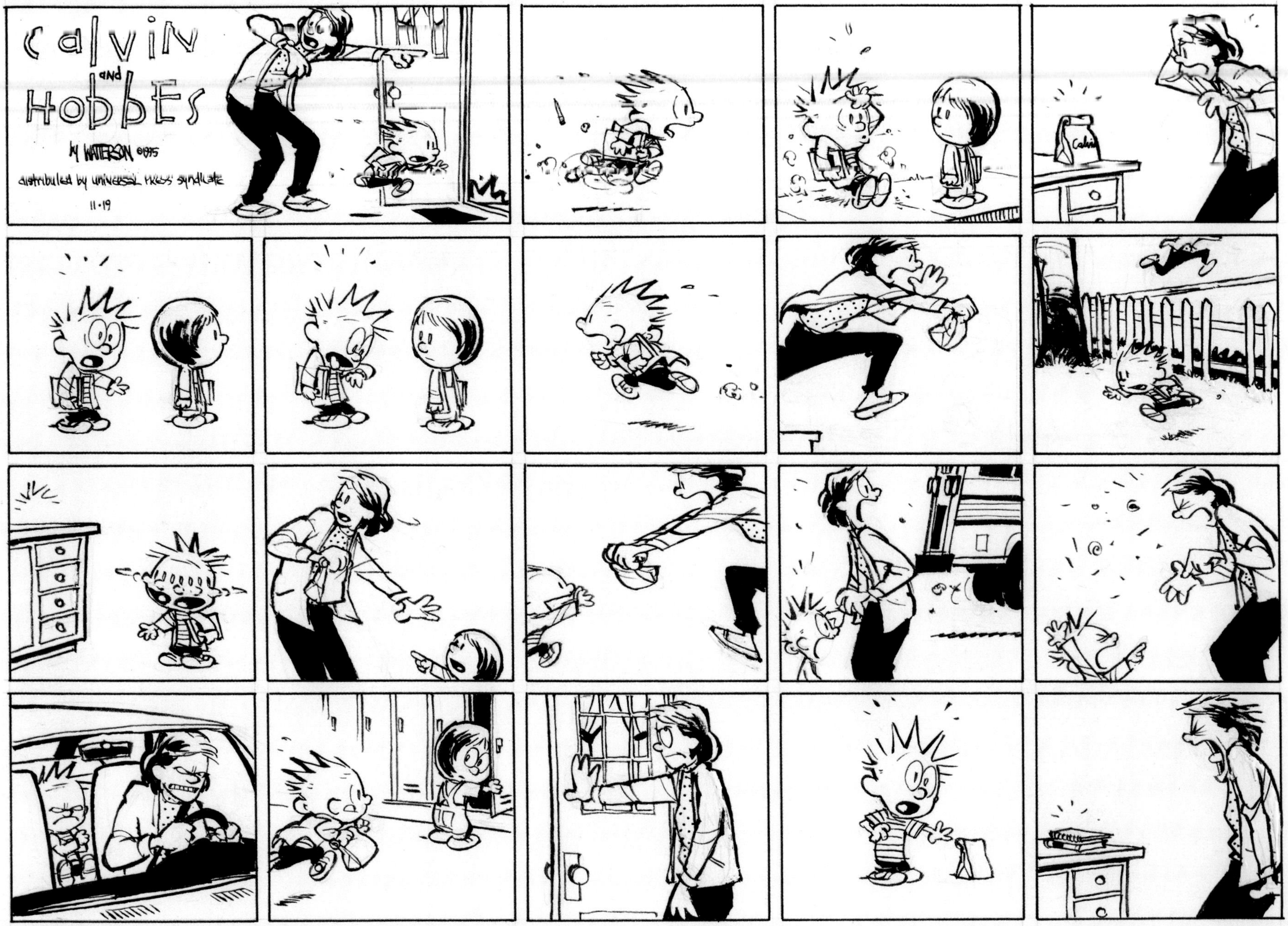
Calvin and Hobbes
by WATTERSON ©1995
distributed by universal press syndicate
11-19
Calvin

NOVEMBER 19, 1995

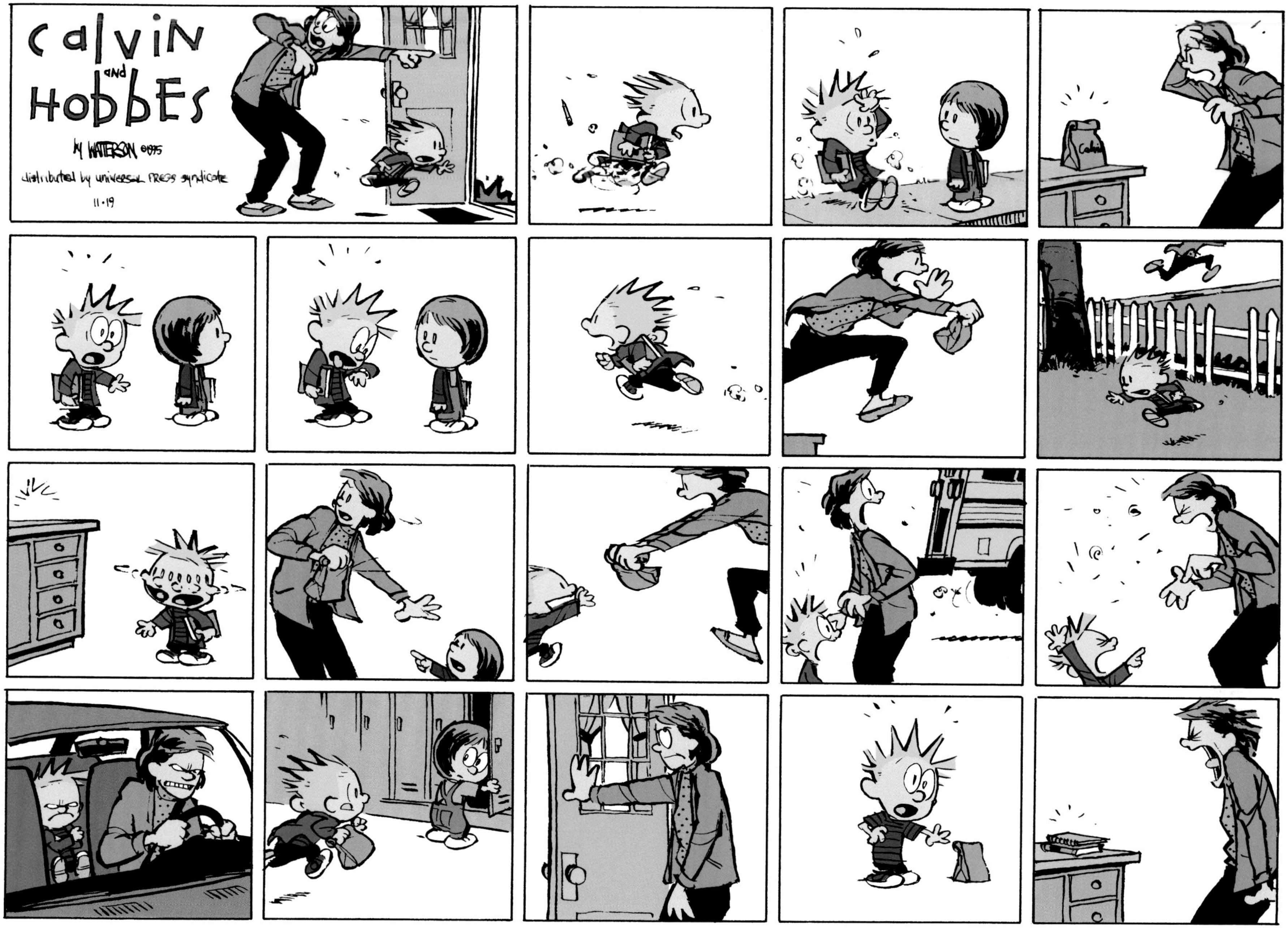
Calvin and Hobbes
by WATTERSON ©1995
distributed by universal press syndicate
11-19

Another strip with no words at all. I kept the panel design extremely clean and simple, so nothing gets in the way of the frantic story. I'm very pleased with how each moment is distilled. A lot of experience fed into each picture by this point.

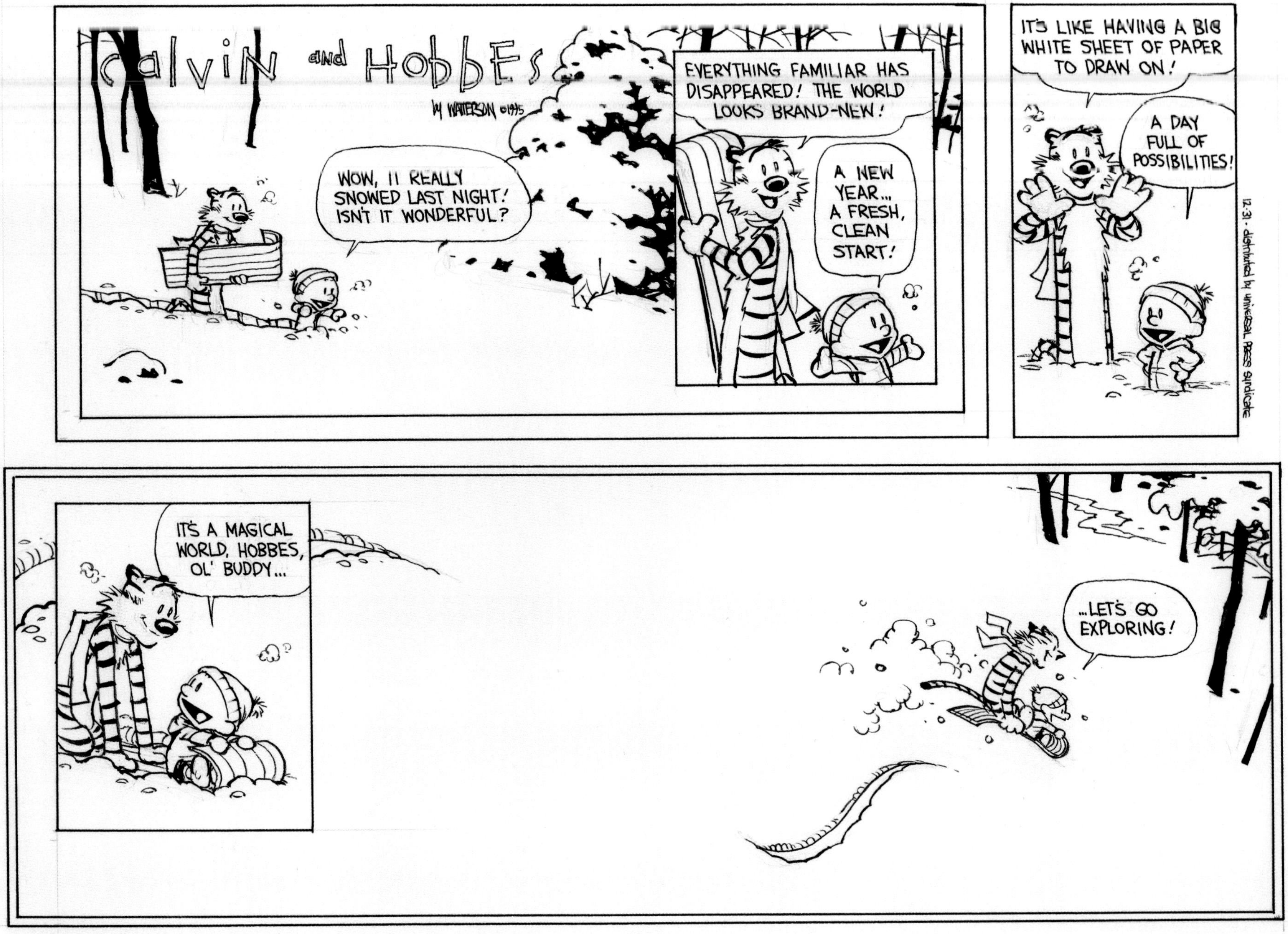
Calvin and Hobbes
by WATTERSON ©1995
WOW, IT REALLY SNOWED LAST NIGHT! ISN'T IT WONDERFUL?
EVERYTHING FAMILIAR HAS DISAPPEARED! THE WORLD LOOKS BRAND-NEW!
A NEW YEAR... A FRESH, CLEAN START!
IT'S LIKE HAVING A BIG WHITE SHEET OF PAPER TO DRAW ON!
A DAY FULL OF POSSIBILITIES!
12-31 · distributed by universal press syndicate
IT'S A MAGICAL WORLD, HOBBES, OL' BUDDY...
...LET'S GO EXPLORING!

DECEMBER 31, 1995

This was the final strip of *Calvin and Hobbes*. I typically colored panel borders and word balloons, but in this strip, I left everything white. Only the characters and the sled were colored, so the drawing would have a very spare and open look to mirror the ideas in the dialogue.

SELECTED BIBLIOGRAPHY

Calvin and Hobbes comic strips by Bill Watterson were collected and reprinted in the following volumes, all of which were published by Andrews McMeel Publishing:

Calvin and Hobbes. 1987.
Something Under the Bed Is Drooling. 1988.
The Essential Calvin and Hobbes. 1988.
Yukon Ho! 1989.
The Calvin and Hobbes Lazy Sunday Book. 1989.
Weirdos from Another Planet! 1990.
The Authoritative Calvin and Hobbes. 1990.
Scientific Progress Goes "Boink." 1991.
The Revenge of the Baby-Sat. 1991.
The Indispensable Calvin and Hobbes. 1992.
Attack of the Deranged Mutant Killer Monster Snow Goons. 1992.
The Days Are Just Packed. 1993.
Homicidal Psycho Jungle Cat. 1994.
The Calvin and Hobbes Tenth Anniversary Book. 1995.
There's Treasure Everywhere. 1996.
It's a Magical World. 1996.

Additional information about Bill Watterson and his work may be found in the following:

Richard Marschall. "Oh, You Kid: A Strip of Leviathan Quality, *The Comics Journal* 127 (February 1989), 72-77.
Bill Watterson. "Calvin and Hobbes," CARTOONIST PROfiles 68 (December 1985), 36-41.
———. "Some Thoughts on *Pogo* and Comic Strips Today," CARTOONIST PROfiles 80 (December 1988), 12-19.
———. "The Cheapening of the Comics," *The Comics Journal* 137 (September 1990), 93-98.
Richard Samuel West. "Interview: Bill Watterson," *The Comics Journal* 127 (February 1989), 56-71.
———. "Errors and Misconceptions," *The Comics Journal* 130 (July 1989), 52.